Making Words Fourth Grade

50 Hands-On Lessons for Teaching Prefixes, Suffixes, and Roots

Patricia M. Cunningham

Wake Forest University

Dorothy P. Hall

Wake Forest University

Boston • New York • San Francisco
Mexico City • Montreal • Toronto • London • Madrid • Munich • Paris
Hong Kong • Singapore • Tokyo • Cape Town • Sydney

Executive Editor: Aurora Martínez Ramos
Series Editorial Assistant: Kara Kikel
Marketing Manager: Danae April
Production Editor: Annette Joseph
Editorial Production Service: Lynda Griffiths
Composition Buyer: Linda Cox
Manufacturing Buyer: Linda Morris
Electronic Composition: Denise Hoffman
Interior Design: Denise Hoffman
Cover Designerr: Kristina Mose-Libon

For Professional Development resources, visit www.allynbaconmerrill.com.

Between the time website information is gathered and then published, it is not unusual for some sites to have closed. Also, the transcription of URLs can result in typographical errors. The publisher would appreciate notification where these errors occur so that they may be corrected in subsequent editions.

ISBN-10: 0-205-58092-0
ISBN-13: 978-0-205-58092-7

Printed in the United States of America

10 9 8 7 6 5 4 3 2 1   BRG   12 11 10 09 08

Photos: Dorothy P. Hall.

Allyn & Bacon
is an imprint of

www.pearsonhighered.com

Pat   Dottie

Patricia M. Cunningham

From the day I entered first grade, I knew I wanted to be a first-grade teacher. In 1965, I graduated from the University of Rhode Island and began my teaching career teaching first grade in Key West, Florida. For the next several years, I taught a variety of grades and worked as a curriculum coordinator and special reading teacher in Florida and Indiana. From the very beginning, I worried about the children who struggled in learning to read and so I devised a variety of alternative strategies to teach them to read. In 1974, I received my Ph.D. in Reading Education from the University of Georgia.

I developed the Making Words activity while working with Title I teachers in North Carolina, where I was the Director of Reading for Alamance County Schools. I have been the Director of Elementary Education at Wake Forest University in Winston-Salem, North Carolina, since 1980 and have worked with numerous teachers to develop hands-on, engaging ways to teach phonics and spelling. In 1991, I wrote *Phonics They Use: Words for Reading and Writing,* which is currently available in its fifth edition. Along with Richard Allington, I also wrote *Classrooms That Work* and *Schools That Work.*

Dottie Hall and I have worked together on many projects. In 1989, we began developing the Four Blocks Framework, a comprehensive approach to literacy that is used in many schools in the United States and Canada. Dottie and I have produced many books together, including the first *Making Words* books and the *Month by Month Phonics* books. These *Making Words* for grade levels kindergarten to fifth grade are in response to requests by teachers across the years to have Making Words lessons with a scope and sequence tailored to their various grade levels. We hope you and your students will enjoy these Making Words lessons and we would love to hear your comments and suggestions.

Dorothy P. Hall

I always wanted to teach young children. After graduating from Worcester State College in Massachusetts, I taught first and second grades. Two years later, I moved to North Carolina, where I continued teaching in the primary grades. Many children I worked with in the newly integrated schools struggled in learning to read. Wanting to increase my knowledge, I received my M.Ed. and Ed.D. in Reading from the University of North Carolina at Greensboro. I also worked at Wake Forest University, where I met and began to work with Pat Cunningham.

After three years of teaching at the college level I returned to the public schools and taught third and fourth grades and served as a reading and curriculum coordinator for my school district. At this time Pat Cunningham and I began to collaborate on a number of projects. In 1989, we developed the Four Blocks Framework, a comprehensive approach to literacy in grades 1, 2, and 3, which we called Big Blocks. Later, we expanded the program to include kindergarten, calling it Building Blocks. By 1999, Pat and I had written four *Making Words* books, a series of *Month by Month Phonics* books, and *The Teacher's Guide to Four Blocks*, and I retired from the school system to devote more time to consulting and writing. I also went back to work at Wake Forest University, where I taught courses in reading, children's literature, and language arts instruction for elementary education students.

Today, I am Director of the Four Blocks Center at Wake Forest University and enjoy working with teachers and administrators around the country presenting workshops on Four Blocks, Building Blocks, guided reading strategies, and phonics instruction. I have also written several books with teachers. One request Pat and I have had for a number of years is to revise the *Making Words* by grade level and include a scope and sequence for the phonics instruction taught. Here it is—Enjoy!

Our thanks to those who reviewed *Making Words Fourth Grade:* Marie Daniel, Clemmons Elementary; Cheryl Dick, Nixa R-II School District; Amy Martindale Kelly, Grantham School; and Betty Pendley, Clemmons Elementary.

Contents

Contents

Introduction

Many teachers first discovered Making Words in the first edition of *Phonics They Use*, which was published in 1991. Since then, teachers around the world have used Making Words lessons to help students discover how our spelling system works. Making Words lessons are an example of a type of instruction called guided discovery. In order to truly learn and retain strategies, students must discover them. But many students do not make discoveries about words on their own. In Making Words lessons, students are guided to make those discoveries.

Making Words is a popular activity with both teachers and students. Students love manipulating letters to make words and figuring out the secret word that can be made with all the letters. While students are having fun making words, they are also learning important information about phonics and spelling. As students manipulate the letters to make the words, they learn how small changes, such as changing just one letter or moving the letters around, result in completely new words.

Teaching a Making Words Lesson

Every Making Words lesson has three parts. First, students manipulate the letters to *make* words. This part of the lesson uses a spelling approach to help students learn letter sounds and how to segment words and blend letters. In the second part of the lesson, students *sort* words according to related words and rhyming patterns. We end each lesson by helping students *transfer* what they have learned to reading and spelling new words. Students learn how the related words and rhyming words they sorted help them read and spell lots of other words.

Each Making Words lesson begins with short, easy words and moves to longer, more complex words. The last word is always the secret word—a word that can be made with all the letters. As students arrange the letters, a student who has successfully made a word manipulates the pocket-chart letters or overhead transparency letters to make the word. Students who don't have the word made correctly quickly fix their word so that they're ready for the next word. The small changes between most words encourages even those students who have not made a word perfectly to fix it because they soon realize that having the current word correctly spelled increases their chances of spelling the next word correctly. In fourth grade, each lesson includes 15 to 20 words, including the secret word that can be made with all the letters.

In Part Two of a Making Words lesson, students sort the words into patterns. Many students discover patterns just through making the words in the carefully sequenced order, but some students need more explicit guidance. This guidance happens when all the words have been made and the teacher guides the students to sort them into patterns. In fourth grade, they sort for two patterns—related words and rhyming words. Some lessons contain homophones—words that sound alike but are spelled differently and have different meanings. The students also sort these and talk about the different meanings of the words.

Many students know letter sounds and patterns but do not apply these to decode an unknown word encountered during reading or to spell a word they need while writing. This is the reason that every Making Words lesson ends with a transfer step. After words are sorted according to related words, students are guided to spell new words based on these related words. When the words are sorted according to rhyme, students use these rhyming words to spell other words. Here is an example of how you might conduct a Making Words lesson and cue the students to the changes and words you want them to make. (This lesson is #29 in *Making Words Fourth Grade*.)

Beginning the Lesson

The students all have a letter strip with these letters: **a a e i d p p r s**
These same letters are displayed in a pocket chart or on plastic tiles on the overhead. Students tear the letters apart and line them up on their desks.

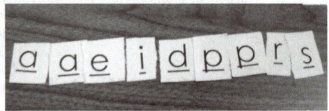

The words the students are going to make are written on index cards. These words will be used for the Sort and Transfer parts of the lesson.

Part One • Making Words

The teacher begins the lesson by telling students what word to make and how many letters each word takes.

> "Use 3 letters to spell the word **sip**. I took a little **sip** of my hot chocolate to make sure it wasn't too hot."

Find someone with **sip** spelled correctly and send that student to spell **sip** with the pocket chart or transparency letters.

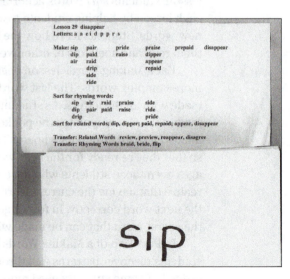

> "Change just the first letter to spell **dip**. It was a sweltering hot day and we took a quick **dip** into the pool to cool off."

> "Start over and use 3 letters to spell **air**. We need to put **air** in our bikes' tires before we can ride."

"Add 1 letter to **air** to spell **pair**. I bought a new **pair** of boots."

"Change 1 letter in **pair** to spell **paid**. I **paid** all my bills."

"Change 1 letter in **paid** to spell **raid**. The hostages were freed during an early morning **raid** on the base."

"Use 4 letters to spell **drip**. The plumber fixed the faucet so it doesn't **drip**."

"Use 4 letters again to spell **side**. Which **side** of the field are you sitting on?"

(Quickly send someone with the correct spelling to make the words with the pocket chart or overhead letters. Keep the pace brisk. Do not wait until everyone has **side** spelled with their letters. It is fine if some students are making **side** as **side** is being spelled with the big letters. Choose your struggling readers to go to the pocket chart when easy words are being spelled and your advanced readers when harder words are being made.)

"Change 1 letter in **side** to spell **ride**. Did you ever **ride** a horse?"

"Add 1 letter to **ride** to spell **pride**. We work hard on our writing and take **pride** in the books we publish."

"Use 5 letters to spell **raise**. In the morning we **raise** the flag."

"Add 1 letter to **raise** to spell **praise**. After the concert, the whole school was full of **praise** for the band and chorus."

"Use 6 letters to spell **dipper**. Mom used a **dipper** to serve the punch."

"Use 6 letters to spell **appear**. I looked up and saw a rainbow **appear** in the sky."

"Use 6 letters to spell **repaid**. My friend got a job and **repaid** me the money I had loaned him."

"Add 1 letter to **repaid** to spell **prepaid**. When I went to pay for the tickets, I discovered my mom had **prepaid** them as a birthday gift."

"I have just one word left. It is the secret word you can make with all your letters. See if you can figure it out."

(Give the students one minute to figure out the secret word. Then give clues if needed. "Our secret word today is related to the word **appear**.")

Let someone who figures it out go to the big letters and spell the secret word—
disappear.

Part Two • Sort Words into Patterns

Using the index cards with words you made, place them in the pocket chart as the students pronounce and chorally spell each. Give them a quick reminder of how they made these words:

"First we spelled a 3 letter word **sip, s-i-p.**"

"We changed the first letter to spell **dip, d-i-p.**"

"We used 3 letters to spell **air, a-i-r.**"

"We added a letter to spell **pair, p-a-i-r.**"

"We changed the last letter to spell **paid, p-a-i-d.**"

"We changed the first letter to spell **raid, r-a-i-d.**"

"We used 4 letters to spell **drip, d-r-i-p.**"

"We used 4 letters to spell **side, s-i-d-e.**"

"We changed the first letter to spell **ride, r-i-d-e.**"

"We added 1 letter to spell **pride, p-r-i-d-e.**"

"We used 5 letters to spell **raise, r-a-i-s-e.**"

"We added 1 letter to spell **praise, p-r-a-i-s-e.**"

"We used 6 letters to spell **dipper, d-i-p-p-e-r.**"

"We used 6 letters to spell **appear, a-p-p-e-a-r.**"

"We used 6 letters to spell **repaid, r-e-p-a-i-d.**"

"We added 1 letter to spell **prepaid, p-r-e-p-a-i-d.**"

"Finally, we spelled the secret word with all our letters, **disappear**, **d-i-s-a-p-p-e-a-r.**"

Sort Related Words

Draw the students' attention to the words on the index cards and remind them that related words are words that share a root word and meaning. Choose a set of related words and model for the students how to use those words in sentences to show how they are related. (Choose the most complex set of words to model.)

paid   repaid   prepaid

"I forgot my wallet, so my friend **paid** for my lunch. I **repaid** him the money I owed the next day. When I went to visit my mom for a month, I **prepaid** all my bills so they wouldn't be overdue when I got back."

"**Re** is a prefix that sometimes means back. If the money was repaid, it was paid back. **Pre** is a prefix that sometimes means before. If the bills were prepaid, they were paid before they were due."

Let volunteers choose other sets of related words and help them construct sentences and explain how the prefixes and suffixes change the root words.

dip   dipper

"A **dipper** is a thing you can use to **dip** things out. **Er** is a suffix that sometimes means the thing that does something."

appear   disappear

"On a cloudy day the sun will suddenly **appear** and then **disappear.**

Dis is a prefix that sometimes makes a word mean the opposite."

Sorting the related words, using sentences that show how they are related, and explaining how prefixes and suffixes affect meaning or change how words can be used in a sentence is a crucial part of each Making Words lesson in fourth grade. Students often need help in explaining how the prefixes and suffixes work.

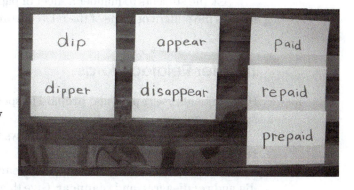

Sort Rhyming Words

Take one of each set of rhymes and place them to form columns in the pocket chart.

sip   air   raid   praise   ride

Have five students find the rhymes and place them under the words you pulled out.

sip	air	raid	praise	ride
dip	pair	paid	raise	side
drip				pride

Have the students read the rhyming words and confirm that they rhyme and have the same spelling pattern.

Part Three • Transfer

The transfer step is the most important part of the lesson because it is when we teach students how rhymes, prefixes, suffixes, and roots help them read and spell lots of other words. Once we have sorted all the words into related words and rhymes, we say several new words and have students decide which word parts these words share with our related words and how they will help the students spell them. Finally, we say several words that rhyme with the rhyming words we made and use the rhyming patterns to spell these. It is very important to make this a learning experience rather than a test. Make sure everyone agrees how to spell the new words before letting anyone write the word.

Ask the students to number a sheet of paper from 1 to 7. Pronounce a word that follows the pattern of some of the related words.

Transfer Related Words

Have students use **repaid** and **prepaid** to spell **review** and **preview**. Give them help to spell the root word if needed.

Let volunteers say a sentence that shows the meaning relationship between **view,** **review,** and **preview.**

Have students use **repaid** and **disappear** to spell two other words that begin with **dis** and **re: disagree** and **reappear.** Give them help to spell the root words if needed.

Let volunteers say a sentence that shows the meaning relationship between **agree** and **disagree** and between **appear** and **reappear.**

Transfer Rhyming Words

Have the students spell these words using the rhyming words to determine the spelling pattern.

glide   braid   clip

We hope this sample lesson has helped you see how a fourth-grade Making Words lesson works and how Making Words lessons help fourth-graders learn how related words and rhyming words help them spell lots of other words.

> Zachary B.
> 1. review
> 2. preview
> 3. re appear
> 4. disagree
> 5. braid
> 6. bride
> 7. flip

Spelling and Decoding Skills Taught in Making Words Fourth-Grade Lessons

Making Words Fourth Grade contains 50 lessons that teach the rhyming patterns, prefixes, suffixes, and roots that fourth-graders need. As students learn to decode and spell words with these prefixes and suffixes, they also learn how these prefixes and suffixes change the meanings of words and how these words are used in sentences. The common prefixes taught in *Making Words Fourth Grade* are:

un, meaning not or opposite (unhappy, unfinished)

in/im, meaning not or opposite (incorrect, impossible)

dis, meaning not or opposite (disappear, disagree)

re, meaning back or again (return, rewrite)

pre, meaning before (prepaid, preview)

under, meaning under or less (underweight, underestimate)

over, meaning over or more (overweight, overestimate)

Suffixes sometimes change meanings of words and sometimes change how the word can be used in a sentence. Often, when a suffix is added, the root word has a spelling change. Spelling changes—consonant doubling, **y** changing to **i** and dropping **e**—should be pointed out to students during the sorting and transfer parts of each lesson if students still need support in consistently applying these spelling changes in their writing. The common suffixes taught are:

er/est, meaning more/most (happier, happiest)

ful, meaning full or with (careful, meaningful)

less, meaning less or without (careless, meaningless)

able/ible, meaning able to (removable, visible)

er/or, meaning person or thing that does something (reporter, computer, inventor)

Some suffixes change how a word can be used in a sentence or the part of speech. The common grammatical suffixes taught are:

ment, changing part of speech (enjoyment, government)

ness, changing part of speech (kindness, happiness)

tion/sion, changing part of speech (pollution, confusion)

ous, changing part of speech (dangerous, mysterious)

y, changing part of speech (bumpy, sunny)

en, changing part of speech (broken, sadden)

al, changing part of speech (musical, national)

ly, changing part of speech (dangerously, mysteriously)

There are other prefixes and suffixes that occur less frequently. Related words containing these suffixes are included in lessons and sorted for but these less common prefixes and suffixes are not the focus of the lesson.

In addition to the common prefixes and suffixes, all lessons contain rhyming words that help students review the more complex vowel patterns. Some lessons contain common homophones. Including homophones, prefixes, suffixes, spelling changes, and complex rhyming patterns allows fourth-graders at all levels to make progress in their spelling and decoding ability. Making Words is truly a multilevel approach in which all students can experience success and learn something new.

Organizing to Teach Making Words

The materials you need to teach a Making Words lesson are quite simple. You need a pocket chart in which to display the word correctly made with the pocket-chart letters. You need a set of pocket-chart or overhead letters big enough for all the students to see. You also need index cards on which to write the words the students will make. Most teachers store their index cards for each lesson in an envelope.

The students need the letters to manipulate. Reproducible letter strips for each lesson are included at the back of this book.

Making Words Homework

Because students like manipulating the letters and coming up with more words than we have time to make in the lesson, a Making Words Take-Home Sheet is a popular activity. You will find a duplicatable template in the back of this book. Write the letters in the boxes at the top in alphabetical order with vowels and then consonants. Student cut or tear the letters apart and fill the boxes with words they can spell with these letters. Encourage them to include words they remember making during the lesson in class and other words they think of.

Lesson 1
fireplaces

Lesson Focus: rhyming patterns **ape**, **ace**, **ice**
re, meaning back or again

Letters:

a	e	e	i	c	f	l	p	r	s

 Make Words: ape ace ice rice race face pace/cape fire seal place
space spice escape reseal replace fireplaces

Directions: Tell the students how many letters to use to make each word.

- Emphasize how changing a few letters or rearranging letters makes different words. Words that can be spelled with the same letters are indicated by a /.

- Give meaning or sentence clues to clarify the word the students are making:

    "Add 1 letter to **ice** to spell **rice**. Do you like **rice**?"

    "Change 1 letter in **space** to spell **spice**. Cinnamon is a **spice**."

    "Use the same letters in **pace** to spell **cape**. Batman wore a **cape**."

    "Use 6 letters to spell **reseal**. I forgot to put the check in the envelope so I had to open it and use tape to **reseal** it."

- Give the students one minute to figure out the secret word and then give clues if needed:

    "Our secret word is a compound word and we spelled both root words."

Sort Rhyming and Related Words

- Have students pronounce words as you put them in the pocket chart. Then have them sort rhyming words and related words.

Rhyming Words:

ape	ace	ice
cape	race	rice
escape	place	spice
	space	
	face	
	pace	

Related Words: seal, reseal; place, replace; fire, place, fireplaces

- Use related words in a sentence that shows relationship.
- Point out how the prefix **re** means back or again in these words.

9

Transfer Related Words

- Have students use **reseal** and **replace** to spell **remove**, **return**, and **react**.
- Ask volunteers to use words in sentences to show the "back or again" meaning of **re**.

Transfer Rhyming Patterns

- Have students use rhyming words to spell **trace**, **price**, and **scrape**.

Lesson 2

treasures

Lesson Focus: rhyming patterns **at, eat, ate, ue**
er/est, meaning more/most
re, meaning back or again

Letters:
a	e	e	u	r	r	s	s	t

 Make Words: art/rat sat eat/ate use/sue sure seat/east rate truer
surer reuse surest treasures

Directions: Tell the students how many letters to use to make each word.

- Emphasize how changing a few letters or rearranging letters makes different words. Words that can be spelled with the same letters are indicated by a /.

- Give meaning or sentence clues to clarify the word the students are making:

    "Add 1 letter to **sue** to spell **sure**. Are you **sure** he is coming?"

    "Change 1 letter in **rat** to spell **sat**. We **sat** in the front row."

    "Use the same letters in **seat** to spell **east**. The sun rises in the **east**."

    "Use 5 letters to spell **surer**. I would be **surer** he was coming if he had answered my email."

- Give the students one minute to figure out the secret word and then give clues if needed:

    "Our secret word is something you might find in an old chest."

Sort Rhyming and Related Words

- Have students pronounce words as you put them in the pocket chart. Then have them sort rhyming words and related words.

Rhyming Words:
sat	eat	ate	sue
rat	seat	rate	true

Related Words: true, truer; sure, surer, surest; use/reuse

- Use related words in a sentence that shows relationship. Point out how the prefix **re** means "back or again" and the "more/most" meaning of **er/est**.

Transfer Related Words

- Have students use **truer**, **surer**, and **surest** to spell **quicker** and **quickest**.

- Have students use **reuse** to spell **rewrite**.

- Ask volunteers to use words in sentences to show how these prefixes and suffixes change the meaning of root words.

Transfer Rhyming Patterns

- Have students use rhyming words to spell **cheat**, **skate**, and **flat**.

Lesson 3
rattlesnake

Lesson Focus: rhyming patterns **eat**, **east**, **ake**
er/est, meaning more/most

Letters: | a | a | e | e | k | l | n | r | s | t | t |

Make Words: ant eat east/seat neat near lean lake snake treat rattle neater
nearer leaner leanest neatest nearest anteater rattlesnake

Directions: Tell the students how many letters to use to make each word.

- Emphasize how changing a few letters or rearranging letters makes different words. Words that can be spelled with the same letters are indicated by a /.

- Give meaning or sentence clues to clarify the word the students are making:

  "Add 1 letter to **eat** to spell **east**. Georgia is **east** of Alabama."

  "Change 1 letter in **neatest** to spell **nearest**. The Browns live next door and they are my **nearest** neighbors."

  "Use the same letters in **east** to spell **seat**. I went to the game early to get a good **seat**."

  "Use 8 letters to spell **anteater**. The **anteater** eats ants with his long snout."

- Give the students one minute to figure out the secret word and then give clues if needed:

  "Our secret word is a compound word and you spelled both root words."

Sort Rhyming and Related Words

- Have students pronounce words as you put them in the pocket chart. Then have them sort rhyming words and related words.

Rhyming Words: eat   lake   east
                    neat   snake   least
                    treat
                    seat

Related Words: near, nearer, nearest; neat, neater, neatest; lean, leaner, leanest;
                    ant, eat, anteater; snake, rattle, rattlesnake

- Use related words in a sentence that shows relationship. Talk about the meanings of the compound words and the "more/most" meaning of **er/est**.

Transfer Related Words

- Have students use **er/est** words to spell **shorter**, **taller**, **shortest**, and **tallest**.
- Ask volunteers to use words in sentences to show the "more and most" meaning of **er/est** .

Transfer Rhyming Patterns

- Have students use rhyming words to spell **beast**, **feast**, and **flake**.

12

Lesson 4

teachers/cheaters (2 secret words)

Lesson Focus: rhyming patterns **eat**, **each**
er, meaning person or thing
re, meaning back or again

Letters: | a | e | e | c | h | r | s | t |

 Make Words: act eat heat each reach teach/cheat react secret
heater/reheat eaters reaches teaches teachers/cheaters

Directions: Tell the students how many letters to use to make each word.

- Emphasize how changing a few letters or rearranging letters makes different words. Words that can be spelled with the same letters are indicated by a /.

- Give meaning or sentence clues to clarify the word the students are making:

    "Add 1 letter to **each** to spell **reach**. Can you **reach** up and get the book off that top shelf?"

    "Use the same letters in **heater** to spell **reheat**. I will **reheat** the soup for lunch."

    "Use 5 letters to spell **react**. We all watched to see how the boy would **react** to the news that his dog had been found."

    "Today's letters spell 2 secret words. See if you can figure them out."

- Give the students one minute to figure out the secret words and then give clues if needed:

    "Our secret words are related to the words **cheat** and **teach**."

 ## Sort Rhyming and Related Words

- Have students pronounce words as you put them in the pocket chart. Then have them sort rhyming words and related words.

Rhyming Words:

eat	each	eaters	reaches
heat	teach	cheaters	teaches
cheat	reach		

Related Words: act, react; eat, eaters; heat, reheat, heater; reach, reaches; cheat, cheaters; teach, teaches, teachers

- Use related words in a sentence that shows relationship. Point out how the prefix **re** means "back or again" and the suffix **er** means "a person or thing that does something."

Transfer Related Words

- Have students use related words to spell **rebuild**, **reprint**, **builder**, and **printer**.
- Ask volunteers to use words in sentences to show how these prefixes and suffixes change the meaning of root words.

Transfer Rhyming Patterns

- Have students use rhyming words to spell **beach**, **peach**, and **peaches**.

Lesson 5
fireworks

Lesson Focus: rhyming patterns **ir**, **ire**, **ise**, **isk**
er, meaning more
er, meaning person or thing
re, meaning back or again

Letters: e i o f k r r s w

Make Words: for fir sir work ~~word~~ sore fire wire wise rise
risk frisk wiser riser worker/rework fireworks

Directions: Tell the students how many letters to use to make each word.

- Emphasize how changing a few letters or rearranging letters makes different words. Words that can be spelled with the same letters are indicated by a /.

- Give meaning or sentence clues to clarify the word the students are making:

  "Add 1 letter to **risk** to spell **frisk**. The police had to **frisk** the suspect to make sure he didn't have any weapons."

  "Change 1 letter in **wiser** to spell **riser**. Are you an early **riser**?"

  "Use the same letters in **worker** to spell **rework**. If you get the wrong answer in math, you need to **rework** the problem."

  "Use 4 letters to spell **sore**. My back was **sore** after I slipped and fell on the ice."

- Give the students one minute to figure out the secret word and then give clues if needed:

  "Our secret word is a compound word and we spelled both root words."

Sort Rhyming and Related Words

- Have students pronounce words as you put them in the pocket chart. Then have them sort rhyming words and related words.

Rhyming Words:

fir	fire	wise	risk	wiser
sir	wire	rise	frisk	riser

Related Words: wise, wiser; work, worker, rework; fire, work, fireworks

- Use related words in a sentence that shows relationship. Point out how the prefix **re** means "back or again," the "person or thing that does something" meaning of **er**, and the "more/most" meaning of **er/est**.

Transfer Related Words

- Have students use **related words** to spell **refill**, **reopen**, and **opener**.
- Ask volunteers to use words in sentences to show how these prefixes and suffixes change the meaning of root words.

Transfer Rhyming Patterns

- Have students use rhyming words to spell **brisk**, **tire**, and **stir**.

Lesson 6
workbench

Lesson Focus: rhyming patterns **oke, eck, ench**
er, meaning person or thing
en, changing part of speech

Letters: | e o b c h k n r w |

 Make Words: no now/own new knew know knob hero woke work neck
wreck owner bench choke broke broken wrench workbench

Directions: Tell the students how many letters to use to make each word.

- Emphasize how changing a few letters or rearranging letters makes different words. Words that can be spelled with the same letters are indicated by a /.

- Give meaning or sentence clues to clarify the word the students are making:

    "Add 1 letter to **broke** to spell **broken**. My CD player is **broken**."

    "Change 1 letter in **knew** to spell **know**. Do you **know** her name?"

    "Use the same letters in **now** to spell **own**. Do you **own** your house or rent it?"

    "Use 6 letters to spell **wrench**. The mechanic used a **wrench** to tighten the bolts."

- Give the students one minute to figure out the secret word and then give clues if needed:

    "Our secret word is a compound word and you spelled both root words."

 Sort Homophones   no, know; new, knew

- Talk about meanings and use in sentences.

Sort Rhyming and Related Words

- Have students pronounce words as you put them in the pocket chart. Then have them sort rhyming words and related words.

Rhyming Words:

woke	neck	bench
broke	wreck	wrench
choke		

Related Words: broke, broken; own, owner; work, bench, workbench

- Use related words in a sentence that shows relationship. Point out the "person or thing that does something" meaning of **er** and how **en** changes how a word can be used in a sentence.

Transfer Related Words

- Have students use related words to spell **giver**, **given**, **driver**, and **driven**.
- Ask volunteers to use words in sentences to show how these prefixes and suffixes change the meaning of root words.

Transfer Rhyming Patterns

- Have students use rhyming words to spell **speck**, **joke**, and **trench**.

Lesson 7
repainted

Lesson Focus: rhyming patterns **aid**, **ied**, **ain**
er, meaning person or thing
re, meaning back or again

Letters: | a | e | e | i | d | n | p | r | t |

 Make Words: pad   paid   raid   edit/diet/tide/tied   tried   train   drain   paint
repaid   retied/dieter   pirate   painted   painter/repaint   repainted

Directions: Tell the students how many letters to use to make each word.

- Emphasize how changing a few letters or rearranging letters makes different words. Words that can be spelled with the same letters are indicated by a /.

- Give meaning or sentence clues to clarify the word the students are making:

 "Add 1 letter to **pad** to spell **paid**. What did you get **paid** for mowing the lawn?"

 "Change 1 letter in **train** to spell **drain**. The runoff water will **drain** into the lake."

 "Use the same letters in **retied** to spell **dieter**. A person on a diet is a **dieter**."

 "Use 6 letters to spell **pirate**. On Halloween, he dressed up as a **pirate**."

- Give the students one minute to figure out the secret word and then give clues if needed:

 "Our secret word is related to the word **paint**."

 ## Sort Homophones   tied, tide

- Use these words in a sentence to show meaning.

Sort Rhyming and Related Words

- Have students pronounce words as you put them in the pocket chart. Then have them sort rhyming words and related words.

Rhyming Words: paid   tied   train
                    raid   tried   drain

Related Words: paid, repaid; tied, retied; paint, painter, painted, repaint, repainted

- Use related words in a sentence that shows relationship. Point out the "person or thing that does something" meaning of **er** and the "back or again" meaning of **re**.

Transfer Related Words

- Have students use related words to spell **refund**, **replant**, **planter**, and **trainer**.
- Ask volunteers to use words in sentences to show how these prefixes and suffixes change the meaning of root words.

Transfer Rhyming Patterns

- Have students use rhyming words to spell **sprain**, **spied**, and **braid**.

Lesson 8

unpleasant

Lesson Focus: rhyming patterns **at**, **ast**, **ent**, **est**, **eal**
un, meaning not or opposite

Letters: | a | a | e | u | l | n | n | p | s | t |

Make Words: at   sat   set   sent/nest   pest   past   last   seal   steal   spent
unseal   unsent   unspent   peanuts   planets   pleasant   unpleasant

Directions: Tell the students how many letters to use to make each word.

- Emphasize how changing a few letters or rearranging letters makes different words. Words that can be spelled with the same letters are indicated by a /.

- Give meaning or sentence clues to clarify the word the students are making:

    "Add 1 letter to **seal** to spell **steal**. The runner was tagged out when he tried to **steal** third base."

    "Change 1 letter in **pest** to spell **past**. I walk **past** the bakery on my way home."

    "Use the same letters in **sent** to spell **nest**. The robin built a **nest** on our porch."

    "Use 8 letters to spell **pleasant**. Yesterday was a sunny, **pleasant** day."

- Give the students one minute to figure out the secret word and then give clues if needed:

    "Our secret word is the opposite of **pleasant**."

Sort Rhyming and Related Words

- Have students pronounce words as you put them in the pocket chart. Then have them sort rhyming words and related words.

Rhyming Words: | at | sent | nest | past | seal |
| sat | spent | pest | last | steal |

Related Words: sent, unsent; seal, unseal; spent, unspent; pleasant, unpleasant

- Use related words in a sentence that shows relationship. Point out that **un** often changes a word to its opposite meaning.

Transfer Related Words

- Have students use related words to spell **unhappy**, **unlucky**, **unfair**, and **unhealthy**.

- Ask volunteers to use words in sentences to show **un** change the meaning to an opposite meaning.

Transfer Rhyming Patterns

- Have students use rhyming words to spell **squeal**, **blast**, and **chest**.

21

Lesson 9

friendly

Lesson Focus: rhyming patterns **y**, **ine**, **ield**
er, meaning person or thing
ly, changing part of speech

Letters: e i d f l n r y

 Make Words: fly fry dry line dine fine deny defy line fine field
yield flier diner finely friend friendly

Directions: Tell the students how many letters to use to make each word.

● Emphasize how changing a few letters or rearranging letters makes different words.

● Give meaning or sentence clues to clarify the word the students are making:

"Change 1 letter in **deny** to spell **defy**. I did not want to **defy** my mom but I really wanted to ride my bike to the game."

"Use 6 letters to spell **finely**. To make coleslaw, you have to chop the cabbage **finely**."

● Give the students one minute to figure out the secret word and then give clues if needed:

"Our secret word is related to the word **friend**."

Sort Rhyming and Related Words

● Have students pronounce words as you put them in the pocket chart. Then have them sort rhyming words and related words.

Rhyming Words:
fly	line	field
dry	fine	yield
fry	dine	
deny		
defy		

Related Words: fly, flier; dine, diner; fine, finely; friend, friendly

● Use related words in a sentence that shows relationship. Point out the "person or thing that does something" meaning of **er** and how **ly** changes how a word can be used in a sentence.

Transfer Related Words

● Have students use related words to spell **boldly**, **strongly**, **carefully**, and **suddenly**.

● Ask volunteers to use words in sentences to show how adding **ly** changes how a word can be used in a sentence.

Transfer Rhyming Patterns

● Have students use rhyming words to spell **shield**, **wield**, and **shine**.

Lesson 10

perfectly

Lesson Focus: rhyming patterns **y**, **ee**, **eel**
re, meaning back or again
ly, changing part of speech
y, changing part of speech

Letters: <u>e</u> <u>e</u> <u>c</u> <u>f</u> <u>l</u> <u>p</u> <u>r</u> <u>t</u> <u>y</u>

Make Words: fly fry try pry prey tree free flee/feel peel feet type
crept creep creepy freely retype perfect perfectly

Directions: Tell the students how many letters to use to make each word.

- Emphasize how changing a few letters or rearranging letters makes different words. Words that can be spelled with the same letters are indicated by a /.

- Give meaning or sentence clues to clarify the word the students are making:

  "Add 1 letter to **creep** to spell **creepy**. Walking down the dark street alone gave me a **creepy** feeling."

  "Change 1 letter in **free** to spell **flee**. The hurricane was coming and residents had to **flee** the coastal towns."

  "Use the same letters in **flee** to spell **feel**. How do you **feel** today?"

  "Use 7 letters to spell **perfect**. Did you ever make a **perfect** score on a test?"

- Give the students one minute to figure out the secret word and then give clues if needed:

  "Our secret word is related to the word **perfect**."

Sort Rhyming and Related Words

- Have students pronounce words as you put them in the pocket chart. Then have them sort rhyming words and related words.

Rhyming Words:

fly	tree	feel
try	free	peel
fry	flee	
pry		

Related Words: crept, creep, creepy; type, retype; free, freely; perfect, perfectly

- Use related words in a sentence that shows relationship. Point out the "back or again" meaning of **re** and how **y** and **ly** change how a word can be used in a sentence.

Transfer Related Words

- Have students use related words to spell **safely**, **quietly**, **boldly**, and **eagerly**.

- Ask volunteers to use words in sentences to show how these prefixes and suffixes change the meaning of root words and how these words are used in sentences.

Transfer Rhyming Patterns

- Have students use rhyming words to spell **wheel**, **spree**, and **dry**.

Lesson 11

playground

Lesson Focus: rhyming patterns **ay**, **oad**, **oud**, **ound**
un, meaning not or opposite
ly, changing part of speech

Letters: a o u d g l n p r y

 Make Words: pay play road load loud aloud proud angry round
ground unload dragon laundry proudly playground

Directions: Tell the students how many letters to use to make each word.

- Emphasize how changing a few letters or rearranging letters makes different words.

- Give meaning or sentence clues to clarify the word the students are making:

    "Add 1 letter to **loud** to spell **aloud**. I read **aloud** the sports article to my little cousin."

    "Change 1 letter in **load** to spell **loud**. That music is too **loud**!"

    "Use 7 letters to spell **laundry**. Who does the **laundry** in your family?"

- Give the students one minute to figure out the secret word and then give clues if needed:

    "Our secret word is a compound word and you spelled both root words."

 ## Sort Rhyming and Related Words

- Have students pronounce words as you put them in the pocket chart. Then have them sort rhyming words and related words.

Rhyming Words:

pay	road	loud	round
play	load	proud	ground
	unload	aloud	playground

Related Words: loud, aloud; load, unload; proud, proudly

- Use related words in a sentence that shows relationship. Point out the "opposite" meaning of **un** and how **ly** changes how a word can be used in a sentence.

 ## Transfer Related Words

- Have students use related words to spell **fairly**, **unfair**, **kindly**, and **unkind**.
- Ask volunteers to use words in sentences to show how these prefixes and suffixes change the meaning of root words.

Transfer Rhyming Patterns

- Have students use rhyming words to spell **cloud**, **clay**, and **hound**.

Lesson 12

underground

Lesson Focus: rhyming patterns **un**, **ude**, **ound**
er, meaning person or thing
re, meaning back or again
un, meaning not or opposite
under, meaning under or less

Letters: e o u u d d g n n r r

 Make Words: go do dog run gun redo undo dude rude round ground
runner gunner dungeon undergo underdog underground

Directions: Tell the students how many letters to use to make each word.

- Emphasize how changing a few letters or rearranging letters makes different words.

- Give meaning or sentence clues to clarify the word the students are making:

    "Add 1 letter to **round** to spell **ground**. Don't eat that cookie after you dropped it on the **ground**."

    "Change 1 letter in **dude** to spell **rude**. The woman was very tired and was **rude** to the salesman who rang the doorbell."

    "Use 8 letters to spell **underdog**. Everyone was shocked that the team that was the **underdog** won the tournament."

- Give the students one minute to figure out the secret word and then give clues if needed:

    "Our secret word is related to the word **ground**."

 ## Sort Rhyming and Related Words

- Have students pronounce words as you put them in the pocket chart. Then have them sort rhyming words and related words.

Rhyming Words: run dude round gunner
gun rude ground runner

Related Words: run, runner; gun, gunner; go, undergo, dog, underdog; ground, underground; do, redo, undo

- Use related words in a sentence that shows relationship. Point out the "person or thing that does something" meaning of **er**, the "under or less" meaning of **under**, the "opposite" meaning of **un**, and the "back or again" meaning of **re**.

Transfer Related Words

- Have students use related words to spell **underline**, **unlined**, **reline**, and **underhand**.

- Ask volunteers to use words in sentences to show how these prefixes and suffixes change the meaning of root words.

Transfer Rhyming Patterns

- Have students use rhyming words to spell **crude**, **pound**, and **found**.

Lesson 13

overtime

Lesson Focus: rhyming patterns **et**, **im**, **ore**
er, meaning person or thing
re, meaning back or again
over, meaning over or more

Letters: | e | e | i | o | m | r | t | v |

 Make Words: met   vet   tie   rim   trim   time   move   more   tore   vote
voter   timer   mover   movie   retie   remove   overtime

Directions: Tell the students how many letters to use to make each word.

- Emphasize how changing a few letters or rearranging letters makes different words.

- Give meaning or sentence clues to clarify the word the students are making:

    "Add 1 letter to **vote** to spell **voter**. A person who votes is a **voter**."

    "Change 1 letter in **move** to spell **more**. Please help yourself to **more** pie."

    "Use 6 letters to spell **remove**. Please **remove** your feet from the table!"

- Give the students one minute to figure out the secret word and then give clues if needed:

    "Our secret word is related to the word **time**."

 ## Sort Rhyming and Related Words

- Have students pronounce words as you put them in the pocket chart. Then have them sort rhyming words and related words.

Rhyming Words: met   rim   more
                     vet   trim   tore

Related Words: vote, voter; move, movie, mover, remove; tie, retie; time, overtime

- Use related words in a sentence that shows relationship. Point out the "person or thing that does something" meaning of **er**, the "back or again" meaning of **re**, and the "over or more" meaning of **over**.

 ## Transfer Related Words

- Have students use related words to spell **overload**, **overhead**, **overdue**, and **overpaid**.

- Ask volunteers to use words in sentences to show how **over** changes the meaning of root words.

Transfer Rhyming Patterns

- Have students use rhyming words to spell **slim**, **snore**, and **score**.

Lesson 14
overweight

Lesson Focus: rhyming patterns **ow, ew, ee, ive**
over, meaning over or more
re, meaning back or again
er, meaning person or thing

Letters: e e i o g h r t v w

 Make Words: grow grew tree hive view vote voter three threw throw
write wrote weigh weight growth review thrive overweight

Directions: Tell the students how many letters to use to make each word.

- Emphasize how changing a few letters or rearranging letters makes different words.

- Give meaning or sentence clues to clarify the word the students are making:

  "Add 1 letter to **weigh** to spell **weight**. I am not telling you my **weight**!"

  "Change 1 letter in **threw** to spell **throw**. **Throw** the ball to me."

  "Use 6 letters to spell **thrive**. My roses **thrive** when they get lots of sun and water."

- Give the students one minute to figure out the secret word and then give clues if needed:

  "Our secret word is related to the word **weigh**."

 ## Sort Rhyming and Related Words

- Have students pronounce words as you put them in the pocket chart. Then have them sort rhyming words and related words.

Rhyming Words: grow   grew   tree   thrive
                    throw   threw   three   hive

Related Words: grow, grew, growth; throw, threw; write, wrote; view, review;
                    vote, voter; weigh, weight, overweight

- Use related words in a sentence that shows relationship. Point out the "person or thing that does something" meaning of **er**, the "back or again" meaning of **re**, and the "over or more" meaning of **over**.

 ## Transfer Related Words

- Have students use related words to spell **oversleep**, **overtired**, **overworked**, and **overpower**.

- Ask volunteers to use words in sentences to show how **over** changes the meaning of root words.

Transfer Rhyming Patterns

- Have students use rhyming words to spell **crew**, **crow**, and **drive**.

Lesson 15
overnight

Lesson Focus: rhyming patterns **orn**, **ote**, **ight**
er, meaning person or thing
en, changing part of speech
over, meaning over or more

Letters: | e | i | o | g | h | n | r | t | v |

 Make Words: horn torn note vote/veto give giver given right night
thorn voter voting govern region overnight

Directions: Tell the students how many letters to use to make each word.

- Emphasize how changing a few letters or rearranging letters makes different words. Words that can be spelled with the same letters are indicated by a /.

- Give meaning or sentence clues to clarify the word the students are making:

    "Add 1 letter to **give** to spell **giver**. The person who gives you something is the **giver**."

    "Change 1 letter in **giver** to spell **given**. I was **given** this ring on my eighteenth birthday."

    "Use the same letters in **vote** to spell **veto**. The governor threatened to **veto** the bill if it passed in the legislature."

    "Use 6 letters to spell **region**. What **region** of the country do we live in?"

- Give the students one minute to figure out the secret word and then give clues if needed:

    "Our secret word is related to the word **night**."

 ## Sort Rhyming and Related Words

- Have students pronounce words as you put them in the pocket chart. Then have them sort rhyming words and related words.

Rhyming Words: horn   note   right
torn   vote   night
thorn

Related Words: vote, voter, voting; give, giver, given; night, overnight

- Use related words in a sentence that shows relationship. Point out the "person or thing that does something" meaning of **er**, the "over or more" meaning of **over**, and how **en** changes how a word can be used in a sentence.

Transfer Related Words

- Have students use related words to spell **overrate**, **overreact**, **overfly**, and **overgrown**.
- Ask volunteers to use words in sentences to show how **over** changes the meaning of root words.

Transfer Rhyming Patterns

- Have students use rhyming words to spell **bright**, **flight**, and **born**.

Lesson 16

inventors

Lesson Focus: rhyming patterns **et, ot, ote, ose, ore, ine**
er, meaning person or thing
or, meaning person or thing

Letters: | e | i | o | n | n | r | s | t | v |

 Make Words: net vet rot not note vote nine vine nose rose/sore
snore voters tennis invent invest investor inventors

Directions: Tell the students how many letters to use to make each word.

- Emphasize how changing a few letters or rearranging letters makes different words. Words that can be spelled with the same letters are indicated by a /.

- Give meaning or sentence clues to clarify the word the students are making:

  "Add 1 letter to **sore** to spell **snore**. Do you **snore** when you are asleep?"

  "Change 1 letter in **invent** to spell **invest**. Do your parents **invest** money for you to go to college?"

  "Use the same letters in **rose** to spell **sore**. I had **sore** feet after the long hike."

  "Use 6 letters to spell **invent**. I think it would be cool to **invent** something totally new."

- Give the students one minute to figure out the secret word and then give clues if needed:

  "Our secret word is related to the word **invent**."

 ## Sort Rhyming and Related Words

- Have students pronounce words as you put them in the pocket chart. Then have them sort rhyming words and related words.

Rhyming Words:

net	rot	note	vine	nose	sore
vet	not	vote	nine	rose	snore

Related Words: vote, voters; invest, investor; invent, inventors

- Use related words in a sentence that shows relationship. Point out the "person or thing that does something" meaning of **er** and **or**.

 ## Transfer Related Words

- Have students use **investor** and **inventors** to spell **actor**, **governor**, **director**, and **visitor**.

- Ask volunteers to use words in sentences to show the "person" meaning of **or**.

Transfer Rhyming Patterns

- Have students use rhyming words to spell **close**, **chose**, and **quote**.

unfortunate

Lesson Focus: rhyming patterns **at**, **ot**
un, meaning not or opposite
en, changing part of speech
er, meaning more

Letters: | a | e | o | u | u | f | n | n | r | t | t |

 Make Words: ran run out fat rat rot trot true after fatter fatten rotten outrun outran untrue nonfat fortune fortunate unfortunate

Directions: Tell the students how many letters to use to make each word.

- Emphasize how changing a few letters or rearranging letters makes different words.

- Give meaning or sentence clues to clarify the word the students are making:

    "Add 1 letter to **rot** to spell **trot**. The horse took off on a fast **trot**."

    "Change 1 letter in **fatter** to spell **fatten**. My dog lost weight when he was sick and I am feeding him extra food to **fatten** him up."

    "Use 7 letters to spell **fortune**. He had the good **fortune** to win tickets to the game."

- Give the students one minute to figure out the secret word and then give clues if needed:

    "Our secret word is related to the word **fortune**."

Sort Rhyming and Related Words

- Have students pronounce words as you put them in the pocket chart. Then have them sort rhyming words and related words.

Rhyming Words: | fat | rot |
| rat | trot |

Related Words: true, untrue; fortune, fortunate, unfortunate; ran, outran; run, outrun; fat, fatter, fatten, nonfat; rot, rotten

- Use related words in a sentence that shows relationship. Point out the "opposite" meaning of **un**, the "more" meaning of **er**, and how **en** changes how a word can be used in a sentence.

Transfer Related Words

- Have students use related words to spell **unlucky**, **unbroken**, **gotten**, and **hidden**.

- Ask volunteers to use words in sentences to show how prefixes and suffixes change the meaning of root words and how words can be used in sentences.

Transfer Rhyming Patterns

- Have students use rhyming words to spell **slot**, **spot**, and **spat**.

Lesson 18
carefully

Lesson Focus: rhyming patterns **ar**, **ear**, **all**
ful, meaning full or with
er, meaning person or thing
re, meaning back or again
ly, changing part of speech

Letters: | a | e | u | c | f | l | l | r | y |

 Make Words: car far ear fear year call fall real care cruel clear
caller/recall really clearly cruelly careful carefully

Directions: Tell the students how many letters to use to make each word.

- Emphasize how changing a few letters or rearranging letters makes different words. Words that can be spelled with the same letters are indicated by a /.

- Give meaning or sentence clues to clarify the word the students are making:

  "Add 1 letter to **ear** to spell **fear**. I have a strong **fear** of snakes!"

  "Change 1 letter in **fear** to spell **year**. The baby is one **year** old."

  "Use the same letters in **caller** to spell **recall**. The store had to **recall** the toys because some of them contained lead paint."

  "Use 5 letters to spell **cruel**. I don't understand how anyone can be **cruel** to animals."

- Give the students one minute to figure out the secret word and then give clues if needed:

  "Our secret word is related to the word **care**."

Sort Rhyming and Related Words

- Have students pronounce words as you put them in the pocket chart. Then have them sort rhyming words and related words.

Rhyming Words:

car	ear	call
far	fear	fall
	year	
	clear	

Related Words: call, caller, recall; real, really; clear, clearly; cruel, cruelly; care, careful, carefully

- Use related words in a sentence that shows relationship. Point out the "person or thing that does something" meaning of **er**, the "back or again" meaning of **re**, the "full or with" meaning of **ful**, and how **ly** changes how a word can be used in a sentence.

Transfer Related Words

- Have students use related words to spell **fearful**, **fearfully**, **cheerful**, and **cheerfully**.
- Ask volunteers to use words in sentences to show how prefixes and suffixes change the meaning of root words and how words can be used in sentences.

Transfer Rhyming Patterns

- Have students use rhyming words to spell **football**, **baseball**, and **basketball**.

Lesson 19

powerfully

Lesson Focus: rhyming patterns **owl**, **ow**, **ew**, **ull**, **ower**
ful, meaning full or with
er, meaning more
ly, changing part of speech

Letters: | e | o | u | f | l | l | p | r | w | y |

 Make Words: owl/low few flew flow/wolf pull full fully lowly lower
power prowl fuller pulley flower powerful powerfully

Directions: Tell the students how many letters to use to make each word.

- Emphasize how changing a few letters or rearranging letters makes different words. Words that can be spelled with the same letters are indicated by a /.

- Give meaning or sentence clues to clarify the word the students are making:

    "Add 1 letter to **full** to spell **fully**. It took four months but the truck driver **fully** recovered from the injuries he got in the accident."

    "Change 1 letter in **lower** to spell **power**. The hurricane had a huge amount of **power** when it came on land."

    "Use the same letters in **flow** to spell **wolf**. Did you ever see a real **wolf**?"

    "Use 6 letters to spell **pulley**. The farmer used a **pulley** to lift the hay bales into the barn loft."

- Give the students one minute to figure out the secret word and then give clues if needed:

    "Our secret word is related to the word **power**."

 ## Sort Rhyming and Related Words

- Have students pronounce words as you put them in the pocket chart. Then have them sort rhyming words and related words.

Rhyming Words: | owl | low | few | pull | power |
| prowl | flow | flew | full | flower |

Related Words: full, fuller, fully; low, lower, lowly; pull, pulley;
power, powerful, powerfully

- Use related words in a sentence that shows relationship. Point out the "more" meaning of **er**, the "full or with" meaning of **ful**, and how **ly** changes how a word can be used in a sentence.

Transfer Related Words

- Have students use related words to spell **hopeful**, **hopefully**, **joyful**, and **joyfully**.

- Ask volunteers to use words in sentences to show how prefixes and suffixes change the meanings of root words and how words can be used in sentences.

Transfer Rhyming Patterns

- Have students use rhyming words to spell **shower**, **growl**, and **howl**.

Lesson 20

powerless

Lesson Focus: rhyming patterns **eep**, **owl**, **ow** (2 sounds)
less, meaning less or without
er, meaning more
er, meaning person or thing

Letters: | e | e | o | l | p | r | s | s | w |

 Make Words: owl/low pow plow slow weep seep lose loser lower
power prowl sleep slower powerless

Directions: Tell the students how many letters to use to make each word.

- Emphasize how changing a few letters or rearranging letters makes different words. Words that can be spelled with the same letters are indicated by a /.

- Give meaning or sentence clues to clarify the word the students are making:

    "Add 1 letter to **pow** to spell **plow**. When the ground thaws, the farmer will **plow** the fields."

    "Change 1 letter in **weep** to spell **seep**. The water began to **seep** through a crack in the wall."

    "Use the same letters in **owl** to spell **low**. The house was in a **low** spot by the river."

    "Use 5 letters to spell **prowl**. The wild animals **prowl** in the forest at night."

- Give the students one minute to figure out the secret word and then give clues if needed:

    "Our secret word is related to the word **power**."

 ## Sort Rhyming and Related Words

- Have students pronounce words as you put them in the pocket chart. Then have them sort rhyming words and related words.

Rhyming Words: (sort according to 2 sounds of **ow**)

owl	low	pow	seep
prowl	slow	plow	sleep

Related Words: lose, loser; low, lower; slow, slower; power, powerless

- Use related words in a sentence that shows relationship. Point out the "person or thing that does something" and the "more" meanings of **er**, and the "less or without" meaning of **less**.

38

Transfer Related Words

- Have students use related words to spell **careless**, **hopeless**, **wireless**, and **helpless**.
- Ask volunteers to use words in sentences to show how **less** changes the meaning of root words.

Transfer Rhyming Patterns

- Have students use rhyming words to spell **sweep**, **sheep**, and **creep**.

Lesson 21

weightless

Lesson Focus: rhyming patterns **eel**, **ile**, **eet**, **ight**
less, meaning less or without

Letters: <u>e</u> <u>e</u> <u>i</u> <u>g</u> <u>h</u> <u>l</u> <u>s</u> <u>s</u> <u>t</u> <u>w</u>

 Make Words: hit   with   wish   heel   tile   while   wheel   sheet   sleet   sweet
light   sight   wishes   weight   hitless   whistle   weightless

Directions: Tell the students how many letters to use to make each word.

- Emphasize how changing a few letters or rearranging letters makes different words.

- Give meaning or sentence clues to clarify the word the students are making:

    "Change 1 letter in **sheet** to spell **sleet**. As it got colder, the rain changed to **sleet**."

    "Change 1 letter in **sleet** to spell **sweet**. Do you like **sweet** things?"

    "Use 7 letters to spell **hitless**. The pitcher pitched a perfect game that left the other team **hitless**."

- Give the students one minute to figure out the secret word and then give clues if needed:

    "Our secret word is related to the word **weight**."

 ## Sort Rhyming and Related Words

- Have students pronounce words as you put them in the pocket chart. Then have them sort rhyming words and related words.

Rhyming Words:

heel	tile	sheet	light
wheel	while	sleet	sight
		sweet	

Related Words: wish, wishes; hit, hitless; weight, weightless

- Use related words in a sentence that shows relationship. Point out the "less or without" meaning of **less**.

 ## Transfer Related Words

- Have students use related words to spell **useless**, **worthless**, **harmless**, and **speechless**.

- Ask volunteers to use words in sentences to show how **less** changes the meaning of root words.

Transfer Rhyming Patterns

- Have students use rhyming words to spell **mile**, **smile**, and **slight**.

Lesson 22

defenseless

Lesson Focus: rhyming patterns **ed, end, eed, ee, ense**
less, meaning less or without

Letters:

e	e	e	e	d	f	l	n	s	s	s

 Make Words: end   fed   see   fee   flee/feel   feed   seed   need   sled   send
    lend   sense   dense   defense   endless   needless   defenseless

Directions: Tell the students how many letters to use to make each word.

- Emphasize how changing a few letters or rearranging letters makes different words. Words that can be spelled with the same letters are indicated by a /.

- Give meaning or sentence clues to clarify the word the students are making:

    "Add 1 letter to **fee** to spell **flee**. As the river flooded, hundreds of people had to **flee** their homes."

    "Change 1 letter in **sense** to spell **dense**. I dreamed I was lost in a large, **dense** forest."

    "Use the same letters in **flee** to spell **feel**. How do you **feel** today?"

    "Use 7 letters to spell **defense**. Our team went for the touchdown but the other team's **defense** was just too strong for us."

- Give the students one minute to figure out the secret word and then give clues if needed:

    "Our secret word is related to the word **defense**."

 ## Sort Rhyming and Related Words

- Have students pronounce words as you put them in the pocket chart. Then have them sort rhyming words and related words.

Rhyming Words:

end	fed	feed	fee	sense
send	sled	seed	flee	dense
		need	see	defense

Related Words: end, endless; need, needless; defense, defenseless

- Use related words in a sentence that shows relationship. Point out the "less or without" meaning of **less**.

 ## Transfer Related Words

- Have students use related words to spell **lawless**, **priceless**, **thoughtless**, and **lifeless**.

- Ask volunteers to use words in sentences to show how **less** changes the meaning of root words.

Transfer Rhyming Patterns

- Have students use rhyming words to spell **tense**, **speed**, and **bleed**.

41

Lesson 23

recyclable

Lesson Focus: rhyming patterns **all, ell, able**
re, meaning back or again
er, meaning person or thing
able, meaning able to
ly, changing part of speech

Letters: | a e e b c c l l r y |

 Make Words: all call ball bell cell real able cable cycle clear
really caller/recall clearly recycle recyclable

Directions: Tell the students how many letters to use to make each word.

- Emphasize how changing a few letters or rearranging letters makes different words. Words that can be spelled with the same letters are indicated by a /.

- Give meaning or sentence clues to clarify the word the students are making:

   "Add 1 letter to **able** to spell **cable**. Do you have **cable** TV?"

   "Change 1 letter in **bell** to spell **cell**. I called her on my **cell** phone."

   "Use the same letters in **caller** to spell **recall**. The company had to **recall** thousand of computers that had faulty batteries."

   "Use 7 letters to spell **recycle**. I try to **recycle** everything I can."

- Give the students one minute to figure out the secret word and then give clues if needed:

   "Our secret word is related to the word **cycle**."

Sort Rhyming and Related Words

- Have students pronounce words as you put them in the pocket chart. Then have them sort rhyming words and related words.

Rhyming Words: all   bell   able
ball   cell   cable
call

Related Words: call, caller, recall; real, really; clear, clearly;
cycle, recycle, recyclable

- Use related words in a sentence that shows relationship. Point out the "person or thing that does something" meaning of **er**, the "back or again" meaning of **re**, the "able to" meaning of **able**, and how **ly** changes how a word can be used in a sentence.

Transfer Related Words

- Have students use related words to spell **washable**, **reliable**, **surely**, and **cleverly**.
- Ask volunteers to use words in sentences to show how suffixes change the meaning of root words and how words can be used in sentences.

Transfer Rhyming Patterns

- Have students use rhyming words to spell **table**, **stable**, and **swell**.

Lesson 24

motorcycles

Lesson Focus: rhyming patterns **oot, ool**
er/est, meaning more/most
er, meaning person or thing
y, changing part of speech

Letters: e o o c c l m r s t y

 Make Words: rot root loot/tool cool room roomy stool scoot close
motor storm stormy soccer cycles closer cooler
coolest scooter motorcycles

Directions: Tell the students how many letters to use to make each word.

- Emphasize how changing a few letters or rearranging letters makes different words. Words that can be spelled with the same letters are indicated by a /.

- Give meaning or sentence clues to clarify the word the students are making:

  "Add 1 letter to **room** to spell **roomy**. The trunk of my new car is quite **roomy**."

  "Add 1 letter to **storm** to spell **stormy**. Sometimes, I like to take walks when the weather is **stormy**."

  "Use the same letters in **loot** to spell **tool**. I put the hammer away in the **tool** box."

  "Use 7 letters to spell **scooter**. Have you ever ridden a **scooter**?"

- Give the students one minute to figure out the secret word and then give clues if needed:

  "Our secret word is a compound word and we made both root words."

 ## Sort Rhyming and Related Words

- Have students pronounce words as you put them in the pocket chart. Then have them sort rhyming words and related words.

Rhyming Words:

root	tool
loot	cool
scoot	stool

Related Words: cool, cooler, coolest; close, closer; room, roomy; storm, stormy; scoot, scooter; cycles, motorcycles

- Use related words in a sentence that shows relationship. Point out the "person or thing that does something" meaning of **er**, the "more/most" meaning of **er/est**, and how **y** changes how a word can be used in a sentence.

44

Transfer Related Words

- Have students use related words to spell **rainy**, **windy**, **sunny**, and **cloudy**.
- Ask volunteers to use words in sentences to show how **y** changes how a word can be used in a sentence.

Transfer Rhyming Patterns

- Have students use rhyming words to spell **pool**, **spool**, and **drool**.

Lesson 25

treatments

Lesson Focus: rhyming patterns **art**, **eat**, **ame**
er/est, meaning more/most
ment, changing part of speech

Letters: | a   e   e   m   n   r   s   t   t   t |

 Make Words: art   eat/ate   mate/meat/tame   same   mean   neat   treat   start
tamer   tamest   meaner   neater   neatest   meanest   treatments

Directions: Tell the students how many letters to use to make each word.

• Emphasize how changing a few letters or rearranging letters makes different words. Words that can be spelled with the same letters are indicated by a /.

• Give meaning or sentence clues to clarify the word the students are making:

"Add 1 letter to **ate** to spell **mate**. Some animals stay with the same **mate** their whole lives."

"Change 1 letter in **tame** to spell **same**. My grandma and I have the **same** birthday."

"Use the same letters in **mate** to spell **meat**. Vegetarians don't eat **meat**."

"Use 7 letters to spell **meanest**. The brothers were angry and tried to think of the **meanest** thing they could do to get back at the person who had lied about them."

• Give the students one minute to figure out the secret word and then give clues if needed:

"Our secret word is related to the word **treat**."

Sort Rhyming and Related Words

• Have students pronounce words as you put them in the pocket chart. Then have them sort rhyming words and related words.

Rhyming Words:
art	eat	tame
start	meat	same
	neat	
	treat	

Related Words: tame, tamer, tamest; mean, meaner, meanest; neat, neater, neatest; treat, treatments

• Use related words in a sentence that shows relationship. Point out the "more/most" meaning of **er/est** and how **ment** changes how a word can be used in a sentence.

Transfer Related Words

- Have students use related words to spell **movement**, **payment**, **shipment**, and **equipment**.
- Ask volunteers to use words in sentences to show how **ment** changes how a word can be used in a sentence.

Transfer Rhyming Patterns

- Have students use rhyming words to spell **flame**, **blame**, and **shame**.

Lesson 26

measurement

Lesson Focus: rhyming patterns **art**, **eat**, **eam**, **ent**
er/est, meaning more/most
ment, changing part of speech

Letters: <u>a</u> <u>e</u> <u>e</u> <u>e</u> <u>u</u> <u>m</u> <u>m</u> <u>n</u> <u>r</u> <u>s</u> <u>t</u>

 Make Words: art   eat   seat/east   sent   rent   mean   smart   amuse   steam   stream
meaner   meanest   eastern   measure   amusement   measurement

Directions: Tell the students how many letters to use to make each word.

- Emphasize how changing a few letters or rearranging letters makes different words. Words that can be spelled with the same letters are indicated by a /.

- Give meaning or sentence clues to clarify the word the students are making:

  "Add 1 letter to **steam** to spell **stream**. We fished in the mountain **stream**."

  "Change 1 letter in **sent** to spell **rent**. We are going to fly to Orlando, **rent** a car, and drive to Disneyworld."

  "Use the same letters in **seat** to spell **east**. The sun rises in the **east** and sets in the west."

  "Use 7 letters to spell **measure**. We use rulers to **measure** things."

- Give the students one minute to figure out the secret word and then give clues if needed:

  "Our secret word is related to the word **measure**."

 ## Sort Rhyming and Related Words

- Have students pronounce words as you put them in the pocket chart. Then have them sort rhyming words and related words.

Rhyming Words:

art	eat	sent	stream
smart	seat	rent	steam

Related Words: mean, meaner, meanest; east, eastern; amuse, amusement; measure, measurement

- Use related words in a sentence that shows relationship. Point out the "more/most" meaning of **er/est** and how **ment** changes how a word can be used in a sentence.

 ## Transfer Related Words

- Have students use related words to spell **pavement**, **government**, **agreement**, and **excitement**.

- Ask volunteers to use words in sentences to show how **ment** changes how a word can be used in a sentence.

Transfer Rhyming Patterns

- Have students use rhyming words to spell **scream**, **chart**, and **gleam**.

Lesson 27

experiments

Lesson Focus: rhyming patterns **ix, ipe, ime, eep**
er/est, meaning more/most
er, meaning person or thing
en, changing part of speech

Letters: e̲ e̲ e̲ i̲ m̲ n̲ p̲ r̲ s̲ t̲ x̲

 Make Words: six mix ripe seep time prime steep mixer exist
ripen ~~riper~~ ripest/stripe expert steeper experiments

Directions: Tell the students how many letters to use to make each word.

- Emphasize how changing a few letters or rearranging letters makes different words. Words that can be spelled with the same letters are indicated by a /.

- Give meaning or sentence clues to clarify the word the students are making:

    "Change 1 letter in **ripen** to spell **riper**. I will eat this banana because it is **riper** than the others."

    "Use the same letters in **ripest** to spell **stripe**. We painted a blue **stripe** along the top of each wall."

    "Use 6 letters to spell **expert**. What topic are you an **expert** on?"

- Give the students one minute to figure out the secret word and then give clues if needed:

    "Our secret word is something we like to do in science."

Sort Rhyming and Related Words

- Have students pronounce words as you put them in the pocket chart. Then have them sort rhyming words and related words.

Rhyming Words: six   ripe   seep   time
mix   stripe   steep   prime

Related Words: ripe, ripen, riper, ripest; mix, mixer; steep, steeper

- Use related words in a sentence that shows relationship. Point out the "more/most" meaning of **er/est**, the "person or thing" meaning of **er**, and how **en** changes how a word can be used in a sentence.

Transfer Related Words

- Have students use related words to spell **tighter**, **tightest**, **tighten**, and **frighten**.

- Ask volunteers to use words in sentences to show the "more/most" meaning of **er/est** and how **en** changes how a word can be used in a sentence.

Transfer Rhyming Patterns

- Have students use rhyming words to spell **gripe**, **grime**, and **crime**.

Lesson 28
dishonesty

Lesson Focus: rhyming patterns **ide, ine, ose**
dis, meaning not or opposite
est, meaning most
y, changing part of speech

Letters: | e i o d h n s s t y |

 Make Words: hid hide side dine dish hose nose nosy noise noisy shine
shiny those dishes honest honesty nosiest dishonest dishonesty

Directions: Tell the students how many letters to use to make each word.

- Emphasize how changing a few letters or rearranging letters makes different words.

- Give meaning or sentence clues to clarify the word the students are making:

    "Add 1 letter to **honest** to spell **honesty**. The cab driver turned in the ring he found in his cab and was rewarded for his **honesty**."

    "Change 1 letter in **shine** to spell **shiny**. I found a new, **shiny** quarter."

    "Use 7 letters to spell **nosiest**. I have the **nosiest** little brother who always wants to know where I am going and what I am going to do."

- Give the students one minute to figure out the secret word and then give clues if needed:

    "Our secret word is related to the word **honest**."

 ## Sort Rhyming and Related Words

- Have students pronounce words as you put them in the pocket chart. Then have them sort rhyming words and related words.

Rhyming Words: hide   hose   shine
side   those   dine

Related Words: hid, hide; nose, nosy, nosiest; noise, noisy; shine, shiny;
dish, dishes; honest, honesty, dishonest, dishonesty

- Use related words in a sentence that shows relationship. Point out the "not or opposite" meaning of **dis**, the "most" meaning of **est**, and how **y** changes how a word can be used in a sentence.

 ## Transfer Related Words

- Have students use related words to spell **bakery**, **discovery**, **recovery**, and **delivery**.

- Ask volunteers to use words in sentences to show how **y** changes how a word can be used in a sentence.

Transfer Rhyming Patterns

- Have students use rhyming words to spell **bride**, **glide**, and **vine**.

Lesson 29

disappear

Lesson Focus: rhyming patterns **ip**, **air**, **aid**, **aise**, **ide**
dis, meaning not or opposite
pre, meaning before
re, meaning back or again
er, meaning person or thing

Letters: | a | a | e | i | d | p | p | r | s |

 Make Words: sip dip air pair paid raid drip side ride pride
raise praise dipper appear repaid prepaid disappear

Directions: Tell the students how many letters to use to make each word.

- Emphasize how changing a few letters or rearranging letters makes different words.

- Give meaning or sentence clues to clarify the word the students are making:

    "Add 1 letter to **raise** to spell **praise**. The woman got **praise** from everyone for rescuing the child who had fallen into the lake."

    "Change 1 letter in **pair** to spell **paid**. The girl got **paid** $10.00 each week for delivering the newspapers."

    "Use 6 letters to spell **repaid**. I borrowed money from my uncle to buy my bike and **repaid** him $5.00 each week."

- Give the students one minute to figure out the secret word and then give clues if needed:

    "Our secret word is related to the word **appear**."

 ## Sort Rhyming and Related Words

- Have students pronounce words as you put them in the pocket chart. Then have them sort rhyming words and related words.

Rhyming Words:

sip	air	raid	praise	side
dip	pair	paid	raise	ride
drip				pride

Related Words: dip, dipper; paid, repaid, prepaid; appear, disappear

- Use related words in a sentence that shows relationship. Point out the "person or thing" meaning of **er**, the "back or again" meaning of **re**, the "before" meaning of **pre**, and the "not or opposite" meaning of **dis**.

Transfer Related Words

- Have students use related words to spell **review**, **preview**, **reappear**, and **disagree**.
- Ask volunteers to use words in sentences to show how prefixes and suffixes change the meanings of root words.

Transfer Rhyming Patterns

- Have students use rhyming words to spell **braid**, **bride**, and **flip**.

Lesson 30

Lesson Focus: rhyming patterns **ad, aid, ive, ave, ove**
dis, meaning not or opposite
er, meaning person or thing
re, meaning back or again
pre, meaning before
over, meaning over or more

Letters: | a | e | i | o | d | p | p | r | s | v |

Make Words: sad   pad   paid   raid   dive   pave   rave   drive/diver   driver
repaid   advise   adviser   approve   prepaid   overpaid   disapprove

Directions: Tell the students how many letters to use to make each word.

- Emphasize how changing a few letters or rearranging letters makes different words. Words that can be spelled with the same letters are indicated by a /.

- Give meaning or sentence clues to clarify the word the students are making:

  "Add 1 letter to **advise** to spell **adviser**. My brother is a math major in college and he has an **adviser** who helps him choose the courses he should take."

  "Change 1 letter in **pave** to spell **rave**. I want to see that movie because all my friends have seen it and given it **rave** reviews."

  "Use the same letters in **drive** to spell **diver**. Would you like to be a deep sea **diver**?"

  "Use 8 letters to spell **overpaid**. The workers went on strike because they thought that they were underpaid and the bosses were **overpaid**."

- Give the students one minute to figure out the secret word and then give clues if needed:

  "Our secret word is related to the word **approve**."

Sort Rhyming and Related Words

- Have students pronounce words as you put them in the pocket chart. Then have them sort rhyming words and related words.

Rhyming Words:

sad	paid	dive	pave	rove	diver
pad	raid	drive	rave	drove	driver

Related Words: drive, driver, drove; dive, diver; advise, adviser; paid, repaid, prepaid, overpaid; approve, disapprove

- Use related words in a sentence that shows relationship. Point out the "person or thing" meaning of **er**, the "back or again" meaning of **re**, the "before" meaning of **pre**, the "not or opposite" meaning of **dis**, and the "over or more" meaning of **over**.

Transfer Related Words

- Have students use related words to spell **disprove**, **distrust**, **dislike**, and **discourage**.
- Ask volunteers to use words in sentences to show how **dis** changes the meaning of a root word.

Transfer Rhyming Patterns

- Have students use rhyming words to spell **slave**, **thrive**, and **grove**.

Lesson 31

Lesson Focus: rhyming patterns **end, ent, ice**
dis, meaning not or opposite
est, meaning most

Letters: | e i o c c d n n s t |

 Make Words: end ice dice nice send tend/dent sent cent nicest/insect intend/indent consent connect disconnect

Directions: Tell the students how many letters to use to make each word.

- Emphasize how changing a few letters or rearranging letters makes different words. Words that can be spelled with the same letters are indicated by a /.

- Give meaning or sentence clues to clarify the word the students are making:

    "Add 1 letter to **ice** to spell **dice**. We use **dice** in lots of board games."

    "Change 1 letter in **sent** that means what you did with a letter to spell **cent** that means one penny. I went to the fair and spent every **cent** I had."

    "Use the same letters in **intend** to spell **indent**. When we start a new paragraph, we **indent** the first sentence."

    "Use 7 letters to spell **consent**. We have to have our parents sign **consent** forms before we can go on fieldtrips."

- Give the students one minute to figure out the secret word and then give clues if needed:

    "Our secret word is related to the word **connect**."

 ## Sort Rhyming and Related Words

- Have students pronounce words as you put them in the pocket chart. Then have them sort rhyming words and related words.

Rhyming Words:

end	ice	dent
send	dice	sent
tend	nice	cent
intend		indent
		consent

Related Words: nice, nicest; connect, disconnect

- Use related words in a sentence that shows relationship. Point out the "most" meaning of **est** and how **dis** changes a word to its opposite meaning.

Transfer Related Words

- Have students use related words to spell **disagreement**, **disappeared**, **disable**, and **disobey**.
- Ask volunteers to use words in sentences to show how **dis** changes the meaning of a root word.

Transfer Rhyming Patterns

- Have students use rhyming words to spell **slice**, **vent**, and **trend**.

independent

Lesson Focus: rhyming patterns **end**, **ent**, **eed**
in, meaning not or opposite
en, changing part of speech

Letters: | e̲ e̲ e̲ i̲ d̲ d̲ n̲ n̲ n̲ p̲ t̲ |

 Make Words: end/den dent deep deed need diet/edit/tied/tide nine deepen
depend intend/indent nineteen dependent independent

Directions: Tell the students how many letters to use to make each word.

- Emphasize how changing a few letters or rearranging letters makes different words. Words that can be spelled with the same letters are indicated by a /.

- Give meaning or sentence clues to clarify the word the students are making:

  "Add 1 letter to **den** to spell **dent**. How did you get that **dent** in your bike?"

  "Change 1 letter in **deed** to spell **need**. The baby is growing and will soon **need** bigger clothes."

  "Use the same letters in **intend** to spell **indent**. Don't forget to **indent** the first sentence of your paragraph."

  "Use 6 letters to spell **depend**. I can always **depend** on my friends for help."

- Give the students one minute to figure out the secret word and then give clues if needed:

  "Our secret word is related to the word **depend**."

 ## Sort Rhyming and Related Words

- Have students pronounce words as you put them in the pocket chart. Then have them sort rhyming words and related words.

Rhyming Words: end   deed   dent
intend need   indent
depend

Related Words: nine, nineteen; deep, deepen; depend, dependent, independent

- Use related words in a sentence that shows relationship. Point out the "not or opposite" meaning of **in** and how **en** changes how a word can be used in a sentence.

 ## Transfer Related Words

- Have students use related words to spell **insane**, **indirect**, **informal**, and **incomplete**.

- Ask volunteers to use words in sentences to show how **in** changes the meaning of a root word.

Transfer Rhyming Patterns

- Have students use rhyming words to spell **spend**, **spent**, and **speed**.

Lesson 33

Lesson Focus: rhyming patterns **oy, oil, one, orn, ice**
in, meaning not or opposite
y, changing part of speech
ly, changing part of speech

Letters: | e | i | o | c | c | l | n | r | r | t | y |

 Make Words: toy   coy   oil   toil   rice   nice   cone   tone   torn   corn   oily
corny   clone   nicely   correct   incorrect   correctly   incorrectly

Directions: Tell the students how many letters to use to make each word.

- Emphasize how changing a few letters or rearranging letters makes different words.

- Give meaning or sentence clues to clarify the word the students are making:

    "Add 1 letter to **oil** to spell **toil**. The farmer had to **toil** in the hot fields all day to get the crop in."

    "Change 1 letter in **cone** to spell **tone**. I could tell by the **tone** of her voice that she was angry."

    "Use 7 letters to spell **correct**. She won $25,000 by giving the **correct** answer to the final question."

- Give the students one minute to figure out the secret word and then give clues if needed:

    "Our secret word is related to the word **correct**."

 ## Sort Rhyming and Related Words

- Have students pronounce words as you put them in the pocket chart. Then have them sort rhyming words and related words.

Rhyming Words:
toy	oil	rice	cone	torn
coy	toil	nice	tone	corn
			clone	

Related Words: oil, oily; corn, corny; nice, nicely; correct, correctly, incorrect, incorrectly

- Use related words in a sentence that shows relationship. Point out the "not or opposite" meaning of **in** and how **y** and **ly** change how a word can be used in a sentence.

Transfer Related Words

- Have students use related words to spell **insanely**, **independently**, **incompletely**, and **incompetent**.
- Ask volunteers to use words in sentences to show how **in** changes the meaning of a root word.

Transfer Rhyming Patterns

- Have students use rhyming words to spell **phone**, **spoil**, and **twice**.

Lesson 34
impatiently

Lesson Focus: rhyming patterns **ay**, **ean**, **ime**, **ame**
im, meaning not or opposite
ment, changing part of speech
ly, changing part of speech

Letters: a e i i l m n p t t y

 Make Words: pay   play   neat   lean   lime   time   tame   name/mean   meanly   neatly   tamely   timely   payment   patient   patiently   impatient   impatiently

Directions: Tell the students how many letters to use to make each word.

- Emphasize how changing a few letters or rearranging letters makes different words. Words that can be spelled with the same letters are indicated by a /.

- Give meaning or sentence clues to clarify the word the students are making:

   "Add 1 letter to **pay** to spell **play**. What games do you like to **play**?"

   "Change 1 letter in **time** to spell **tame**. The birds were very **tame** and ate right out of our hands."

   "Use the same letters in **name** to spell **mean**. She looked at me in a **mean** way."

   "Use 7 letters to spell **patient**. The airplane was delayed because of the terrible weather and we all just had to be **patient**."

- Give the students one minute to figure out the secret word and then give clues if needed:

   "Our secret word is related to the word **patient**."

Sort Rhyming and Related Words

- Have students pronounce words as you put them in the pocket chart. Then have them sort rhyming words and related words.

Rhyming Words:

pay	lean	lime	tame
play	mean	time	name

Related Words: pay, payment; neat, neatly; mean, meanly; time, timely; tame, tamely; patient, impatient, patiently, impatiently

- Use related words in a sentence that shows relationship. Point out the "not or opposite" meaning of **im** and how **ment** and **ly** change how a word can be used in a sentence.

Transfer Related Words

- Have students use related words to spell **improper**, **improperly**, **imperfect**, and **imperfectly**.

- Ask volunteers to use words in sentences to show how **im** changes the meaning of a root word.

Transfer Rhyming Patterns

- Have students use rhyming words to spell **blame**, **flame**, and **shame**.

Lesson 35

Lesson Focus: rhyming patterns **ace**, **are**, **oat**, **oom**, **ame**
able, meaning able to
or, meaning person or thing

Letters:

| a | e | o | o | b | c | f | l | m | r | t |

 Make Words: act ace race/care bare boat foot trace bloom broom float
flame blame actor comfort barefoot footrace comfortable

Directions: Tell the students how many letters to use to make each word.

- Emphasize how changing a few letters or rearranging letters makes different words. Words that can be spelled with the same letters are indicated by a /.

- Give meaning or sentence clues to clarify the word the students are making:

  "Add 1 letter to **ace** to spell **race**. Who won the **race**?"

  "Change 1 letter in **bloom** to spell **broom**. Get the **broom** and sweep up the cereal that spilled."

  "Use the same letters in **race** to spell **care**. She took good **care** of her cat."

  "Use 8 letters to spell **footrace**. We ran in the 10K **footrace**."

- Give the students one minute to figure out the secret word and then give clues if needed:

  "Our secret word is related to the word **comfort**."

Sort Rhyming and Related Words

- Have students pronounce words as you put them in the pocket chart. Then have them sort rhyming words and related words.

Rhyming Words:

ace	care	boat	bloom	flame
race	bare	float	broom	blame
trace				

Related Words: act, actor; comfort, comfortable; bare, foot, barefoot;
race, foot, footrace

- Use related words in a sentence that shows relationship. Point out the "person or thing" meaning of **or** and the "able to" meaning of **able**.

Transfer Related Words

- Have students use related words to spell **workable**, **portable**, **suitable**, and **favorable**.

- Ask volunteers to use words in sentences to show how **able** changes the meaning of a root word.

Transfer Rhyming Patterns

- Have students use rhyming words to spell **gloom**, **gloat**, and **glare**.

Lesson 36

undesirable

Lesson Focus: rhyming patterns **end, ead**
                        able, meaning able to
                        er, meaning person or thing
                        re, meaning back or again
                        un, meaning not or opposite

Letters: | a e e i u b d l n r s |

 Make Words: use end read lead able blend build reuse island
                              leader desire unable blender builder/rebuild reusable
                              islander desirable undesirable

Directions: Tell the students how many letters to use to make each word.

- Emphasize how changing a few letters or rearranging letters makes different words. Words that can be spelled with the same letters are indicated by a /.

- Give meaning or sentence clues to clarify the word the students are making:

  "Change 1 letter in **read** to spell **lead**. Who wants to **lead** the line?"

  "Use the same letters in **builder** to spell **rebuild**. After the storm, the town had to **rebuild** the hospital and the fire station."

  "Use 8 letters to spell **islander**. A person who lives on an island is called an **islander**."

- Give the students one minute to figure out the secret word and then give clues if needed:

  "Our secret word is related to the word **desire**."

 ## Sort Rhyming and Related Words

- Have students pronounce words as you put them in the pocket chart. Then have them sort rhyming words and related words.

Rhyming Words: end   read
                              blend   lead

Related Words: blend, blender; lead, leader; build, builder, rebuild; island, islander; able, unable; use, reuse, reusable; desire, desirable, undesirable

- Use related words in a sentence that shows relationship. Point out the "person or thing" meaning of **er**, the "back or again" meaning of **re**, the "not or opposite" meaning of **un**, and the "able to" meaning of **able**.

Transfer Related Words

- Have students use related words to spell **likable**, **lovable**, **reliable**, and **valuable**. Point out spelling changes.

- Ask volunteers to use words in sentences to show how **able** changes the meaning of a root word.

Transfer Rhyming Patterns

- Have students use rhyming words to spell **spend**, **plead**, and **trend**.

Lesson 37
inflexible

Lesson Focus: rhyming patterns **ine, ile, ill, ell**
ible, meaning able to
in, meaning not or opposite

Letters:

e	e	i	i	b	f	l	l	n	x

Make Words: fix   fin   fine   line   life/file   fill   bill   bell   fell   flex   exile   belief   lifeline   flexible   inflexible

Directions: Tell the students how many letters to use to make each word.

- Emphasize how changing a few letters or rearranging letters makes different words. Words that can be spelled with the same letters are indicated by a /.

- Give meaning or sentence clues to clarify the word the students are making:

  "Add 1 letter to **fin** to spell **fine**. It was a bright, sunny, **fine** day."

  "Change 1 letter in **bill** to spell **bell**. What time does the **bell** ring?"

  "Use the same letters in **life** to spell **file**. Who will help me **file** these papers?"

  "Use 5 letters to spell **exile**. The refugees were living in **exile** in France."

- Give the students one minute to figure out the secret word and then give clues if needed:

  "Our secret word is related to the word **flex**."

Sort Rhyming and Related Words

- Have students pronounce words as you put them in the pocket chart. Then have them sort rhyming words and related words.

Rhyming Words:

fine	fill	bell	file
line	bill	fell	exile

Related Words: life, line, lifeline; flex, flexible, inflexible

- Use related words in a sentence that shows relationship. Point out the "not or opposite" meaning of **in** and the "able to" meaning of **ible**.

Transfer Related Words

- Have students use related words to spell **sensible**, **insensible**, **visible**, and **invisible**.
- Ask volunteers to use words in sentences to show how **in** and **ible** change the meanings of root words.

Transfer Rhyming Patterns

- Have students use rhyming words to spell **grill**, **shine**, and **shell**.

Lesson 38

personal

Lesson Focus: rhyming patterns **ear**, **earn**, **ose**, **ore**
al, changing part of speech

Letters: | a | e | o | l | n | p | r | s |

Make Words: ear near/earn pose nose rose/sore learn spear/spare
snare snore solar reason person personal

Directions: Tell the students how many letters to use to make each word.

- Emphasize how changing a few letters or rearranging letters makes different words. Words that can be spelled with the same letters are indicated by a /.

- Give meaning or sentence clues to clarify the word the students are making:

  "Add 1 letter to **ear** to spell **near**. Is your house **near** the fire station?"

  "Change 1 letter in **spare** to spell **snare**. A **snare** is a trap for catching birds or small animals."

  "Use the same letters in **near** to spell **earn**. What do you do to **earn** your allowance?"

  "Use 6 letters to spell **reason**. What is your **reason** for being late?"

- Give the students one minute to figure out the secret word and then give clues if needed:

  "Our secret word is related to the word **person**."

Sort Rhyming and Related Words

- Have students pronounce words as you put them in the pocket chart. Then have them sort rhyming words and related words.

Rhyming Words:
ear	earn	pose	sore
near	learn	nose	snore
		rose	

Related Words: person, personal

- Use related words in a sentence that shows relationship. Point out how **al** changes how a word can be used in a sentence.

Transfer Related Words

- Have students use related words to spell **musical**, **magical**, **national**, and **logical**.
- Ask volunteers to use words in sentences to show how **al** changes how words can be used in a sentence.

Transfer Rhyming Patterns

- Have students use rhyming words to spell **score**, **shore**, and **chore**.

Lesson 39

electrical

Lesson Focus: rhyming patterns **ice**, **ace**, **all**, **ell**, **ate**
re, meaning back or again
er, meaning person or thing
er, meaning more
al, changing part of speech

Letters: | a e e i c c l l r t |

 Make Words: ice ace all call tall tell cell rice race rate late
later taller teller/retell recall/caller electric electrical

Directions: Tell the students how many letters to use to make each word.

- Emphasize how changing a few letters or rearranging letters makes different words. Words that can be spelled with the same letters are indicated by a /.

- Give meaning or sentence clues to clarify the word the students are making:

    "Add 1 letter to **late** to spell **later**. On weekends we can stay up **later** than we can on school days."

    "Change 1 letter in **tall** to spell **tell**. I did not **tell** anyone the secret."

    "Use the same letters in **teller** to spell **retell**. Can you **retell** the story?"

    "Use 8 letters to spell **electric**. Do you have a gas stove or an **electric** stove?"

- Give the students one minute to figure out the secret word and then give clues if needed:

    "Our secret word is related to the word **electric**."

 ## Sort Rhyming and Related Words

- Have students pronounce words as you put them in the pocket chart. Then have them sort rhyming words and related words.

Rhyming Words: | ice | ace | all | tell | late |
| rice | race | call | cell | rate |
| | | tall | | |

Related Words: late, later; tall, taller; tell, teller, retell; call, recall, caller; electric, electrical

- Use related words in a sentence that shows relationship. Point out the "back or again" meaning of **re**, the "more" and "person" meaning of **er**, and how **al** changes how a word can be used in a sentence.

Transfer Related Words

- Have students use related words to spell **tropical**, **political**, **cultural**, and **natural**.
- Ask volunteers to use words in sentences to show how **al** changes how words can be used in sentences.

Transfer Rhyming Patterns

- Have students use rhyming words to spell **space**, **twice**, and **trace**.

Lesson 40

predictable

Lesson Focus: rhyming patterns **ace, ade, ate, ide**
able, meaning able to
pre, meaning before
re, meaning back or again
al, changing part of speech

Letters: | a̲ e̲ e̲ i̲ b̲ c̲ d̲ l̲ p̲ r̲ t̲ |

 Make Words: act   date   late   rate   race   trade   trace   place   brace   blade
react   pride   bride   bridal   debate   replace   predict   predictable

Directions: Tell the students how many letters to use to make each word.

- Emphasize how changing a few letters or rearranging letters makes different words.

- Give meaning or sentence clues to clarify the word the students are making:

    "Add 1 letter to **race** to spell **trace**. **Trace** the pattern and then cut out your ornament."

    "Change 1 letter in **place** to spell **brace**. The man had to wear a back **brace** for several months after the accident."

    "Use 6 letters to spell **bridal**. My niece is getting married and I helped her pick out her **bridal** gown."

- Give the students one minute to figure out the secret word and then give clues if needed:

    "Our secret word is related to the word **predict**."

 ## Sort Rhyming and Related Words

- Have students pronounce words as you put them in the pocket chart. Then have them sort rhyming words and related words.

Rhyming Words: | date | trade | trace | bride |
|------|-------|-------|-------|
| late | blade | brace | pride |
| debate | | place | |
| rate | | race | |

Related Words: bride, bridal; act, react; place, replace; predict, predictable

- Use related words in a sentence that shows relationship. Point out the "back or again" meaning of **re**, the "able to" meaning of **able**, and how **al** changes how a word can be used in a sentence.

Transfer Related Words

- Have students use related words to spell **favorable**, **desirable**, **unfavorable**, and **undesirable**.

- Ask volunteers to use words in sentences to show how **able** changes the meanings of root words.

Transfer Rhyming Patterns

- Have students use rhyming words to spell **shade**, **slide**, and **glide**.

Lesson 41

dangerous

Lesson Focus: rhyming patterns **our**, **ound**, **age**, **ear**
un, meaning not or opposite
ous, changing part of speech

Letters: | a e o u d g n r s |

 Make Words: do   our   age   rage/gear   dear   sour   does   undo   sound
round   ground   undoes   garden/danger   dangerous

Directions: Tell the students how many letters to use to make each word.

- Emphasize how changing a few letters or rearranging letters makes different words. Words that can be spelled with the same letters are indicated by a /.

- Give meaning or sentence clues to clarify the word the students are making:

  "Add 1 letter to **round** to spell **ground**. The little boy dropped his ice cream cone on the **ground**."

  "Change 1 letter in **sound** to spell **round**. I am looking for a nice, round **pumpkin**."

  "Use the same letters in **garden** to spell **danger**. The firefighter went into the burning building to rescue the dog, putting his own life in **danger**."

  "Use 6 letters to spell **undoes**. Some people think that the one bad decision the coach made **undoes** all the smart things he did in the past."

- Give the students one minute to figure out the secret word and then give clues if needed:

  "Our secret word is related to the word **danger**."

 ## Sort Rhyming and Related Words

- Have students pronounce words as you put them in the pocket chart. Then have them sort rhyming words and related words.

Rhyming Words: | our | age | gear | round |
| | sour | rage | dear | sound |
| | | | | ground |

Related Words: do, undo; does, undoes; danger, dangerous

- Use related words in a sentence that shows relationship. Point out the "not or opposite" meaning of **un** and how **ous** changes the way a word can be used in a sentence.

Transfer Related Words

- Have students use related words to spell **poisonous**, **humorous**, **mountainous**, and **hazardous**.

- Ask volunteers to use words in sentences to show how **ous** changes how words can be used in sentences.

Transfer Rhyming Patterns

- Have students use rhyming words to spell **cage**, **stage**, and **bound**.

Lesson 42

mysteriously

Lesson Focus: rhyming patterns **ue, ess, ile, ime**
ous, changing part of speech
ly, changing part of speech
y, changing part of speech

Letters: | e̲ | i̲ | o̲ | u̲ | l̲ | m̲ | r̲ | s̲ | s̲ | t̲ | y̲ | y̲ |

Make Words: sue   true   sure   mile/lime   less   mess   messy   truly
smile/slime   storm   stormy   sister   serious   mystery
sisterly   seriously   mysterious   mysteriously

Directions: Tell the students how many letters to use to make each word.

- Emphasize how changing a few letters or rearranging letters makes different words. Words that can be spelled with the same letters are indicated by a /.

- Give meaning or sentence clues to clarify the word the students are making:

  "Add 1 letter to **mess** to spell **messy**. Is your room neat or **messy**?"

  "Change 1 letter in **less** to spell **mess**. Whoever made this **mess** needs to clean it up!"

  "Use the same letters in **smile** to spell **slime**. There was a lot of mud and **slime** at the bottom of the pond."

  "Use 7 letters to spell **serious**. Crime is a **serious** problem in many big cities."

- Give the students one minute to figure out the secret word and then give clues if needed:

  "Our secret word is related to the word **mysterious**."

Sort Rhyming and Related Words

- Have students pronounce words as you put them in the pocket chart. Then have them sort rhyming words and related words.

Rhyming Words: | sue | less | mile | lime |
| true | mess | smile | slime |

Related Words: mess, messy; storm, stormy; true, truly; sister, sisterly; serious, seriously; mystery, mysterious, mysteriously

- Use related words in a sentence that shows relationship. Point out how **y**, **ous**, and **ly** change how words can be used in sentences.

Transfer Related Words

- Have students use related words to spell **furious**, **furiously**, **victorious**, and **victoriously**.
- Ask volunteers to use words in sentences to show how **ous** and **ly** change how words can be used in sentences.

Transfer Rhyming Patterns

- Have students use rhyming words to spell **crime**, **press**, and **prime**.

Lesson 43

subtraction

Lesson Focus: rhyming patterns **an, oat, oast**
or, meaning person
tion, changing part of speech

Letters:

a	i	o	u	b	c	n	r	s	t	t

 Make Words: act ran can cast boat coat coast toast actor outran action
auction/caution station suction outcast subtract subtraction

Directions: Tell the students how many letters to use to make each word.

- Emphasize how changing a few letters or rearranging letters makes different words. Words that can be spelled with the same letters are indicated by a /.

- Give meaning or sentence clues to clarify the word the students are making:

  "Add 1 letter to **action** to spell **auction**. We sold our old car at an **auction**."

  "Change 2 letters in **station** to spell **suction**. The old vacuum cleaner didn't have much **suction**."

  "Use the same letters in **auction** to spell **caution**. An orange blinking light means you need to use **caution**."

  "Use 8 letters to spell **subtract**. Can you **subtract** 23 from 100 in your head?"

- Give the students one minute to figure out the secret word and then give clues if needed:

  "Our secret word is related to the word **subtract**."

 ## Sort Rhyming and Related Words

- Have students pronounce words as you put them in the pocket chart. Then have them sort rhyming words and related words.

Rhyming Words:

boat	coast	ran
coat	toast	can

Related Words: act, actor, action; ran, outran; cast, outcast; subtract, subtraction

- Use related words in a sentence that shows relationship. Point out the "person" meaning of **or** and how **tion** changes how words can be used in sentences.

 ## Transfer Related Words

- Have students use related words to spell **direction**, **inspection**, **protection**, and **perfection**.

- Ask volunteers to use words in sentences to show how **tion** changes how words can be used in sentences.

Transfer Rhyming Patterns

- Have students use rhyming words to spell **boast**, **roast**, and **float**.

Lesson 44

celebrations

Lesson Focus: rhyming patterns **ice**, **ean**
er/est, meaning more/most
or, meaning person
re, meaning back or again
tion, changing part of speech

Letters:

| a | e | e | i | o | b | c | l | n | r | s | t |

Make Words: act   ice   nice   lean   clean   react   elect   actor   nicer
nicest   locate   action   leaner   leanest   cleaner   cleanest
reaction   relocate   elections   celebrations

Directions: Tell the students how many letters to use to make each word.

- Emphasize how changing a few letters or rearranging letters makes different words.

- Give meaning or sentence clues to clarify the word the students are making:

  "Add 1 letter to **lean** to spell **clean**. Do you like to **clean** your room?"

  "Use 8 letters to spell **reaction**. What was her **reaction** when you told her the dog was lost?"

  "Use 8 letters to spell **relocate**. We are going to move because my dad's job requires him to **relocate** every five years."

- Give the students one minute to figure out the secret word and then give clues if needed:

  "Our secret word is related to the word **celebrate**."

Sort Rhyming and Related Words

- Have students pronounce words as you put them in the pocket chart. Then have them sort rhyming words and related words.

Rhyming Words: ice   lean
                     nice   clean

Related Words: act, actor, action, react, reaction; elect, elections; lean, leaner, leanest; clean, cleaner, cleanest; nice, nicer, nicest; locate, relocate

- Use related words in a sentence that shows relationship. Point out the "back or again" meaning of **re**, the "person" meaning of **or**, the "more/most" meaning of **er/est**, and how **tion** changes how words can be used in sentences.

Transfer Related Words

- Have students use related words to spell **location**, **vacation**, **migration**, and **creation**.
- Ask volunteers to use words in sentences to show how **tion** changes how words can be used in sentences.

Transfer Rhyming Patterns

- Have students use rhyming words to spell **slice**, **twice**, and **bean**.

Lesson 45

permission/impression (2 secret words)

Lesson Focus: rhyming patterns **in**, **ine**, **ess**
er/est, meaning more/most
sion, changing part of speech
en, changing part of speech

Letters: <u>e</u> <u>i</u> <u>i</u> <u>o</u> <u>m</u> <u>n</u> <u>p</u> <u>r</u> <u>s</u> <u>s</u>

 Make Words: pin   pine   mess   miss   ripe   spin   ripe   spine   ripen   press   person
prison   impress   imprison   emission   remission   permission/impression

Directions: Tell the students how many letters to use to make each word.

- Emphasize how changing a few letters or rearranging letters makes different words. Words that can be spelled with the same letters are indicated by a /.

- Give meaning or sentence clues to clarify the word the students are making:

  "Add 1 letter to **emission** to spell **remission**. My grandma feels fine now because her cancer is in **remission**."

  "Change 1 letter in **mess** to spell **miss**. Do you **miss** your school friends when we have a vacation?"

  "Use 8 letters to spell **emission**. Global warming is caused by the **emission** of carbon dioxide and other gasses into the atmosphere."

  "Today's letters make 2 secret words. See if you can figure out one of them."

- Give the students one minute to figure out the secret words and then give clues if needed:

  "One secret word is related to the word **impress**. The other secret word is related to the word **permit**."

Sort Rhyming and Related Words

- Have students pronounce words as you put them in the pocket chart. Then have them sort rhyming words and related words.

Rhyming Words: pin   pine   mess
spin   spine   press

Related Words: ripe, ripen; prison, imprison; press, impress, impression

- Use related words in a sentence that shows relationship. Point out how **en** and **sion** change how a word can be used in a sentence.

Transfer Related Words

- Have students use related words to spell **expression**, **confession**, **confusion**, and **explosion**.

- Ask volunteers to use words in sentences to show how **tion** changes how words can be used in sentences.

Transfer Rhyming Patterns

- Have students use rhyming words to spell **twin**, **twine**, and **stress**.

Lesson 46

politicians

Lesson Focus: rhyming patterns **oil**, **ail**, **ain**
tion, changing part of speech

Letters: a i i i o c l n p s t

Make Words: cat/act oil soil sail nail pail pain plain stain snail
spoil piano action catnip pianist politics politicians

Directions: Tell the students how many letters to use to make each word.

- Emphasize how changing a few letters or rearranging letters makes different words. Words that can be spelled with the same letters are indicated by a /.

- Give meaning or sentence clues to clarify the word the students are making:

  "Add 1 letter to **pain** to spell **plain**. I like **plain** vanilla ice cream."

  "Change 1 letter in **soil** to spell **sail**. Did you ever **sail** in a sailboat?"

  "Use the same letters in **cat** to spell **act**. Who wants to **act** in our play?"

  "Use 8 letters to spell **politics**. It was almost time for the election and everyone was talking about **politics**."

- Give the students one minute to figure out the secret word and then give clues if needed:

  "Our secret word is related to the word **politics**."

Sort Rhyming and Related Words

- Have students pronounce words as you put them in the pocket chart. Then have them sort rhyming words and related words.

Rhyming Words:

oil	sail	pain
soil	pail	plain
spoil	snail	stain
	nail	

Related Words: act, action; piano, pianist; politics, politicians; cat, catnip

- Use related words in a sentence that shows relationship. Point out the "person" meaning of **ist** and **ian** and how **tion** changes how words can be used in sentences.

Transfer Related Words

- Have students use related words to spell **guitarist**, **scientist**, **librarian**, and **musician**.

- Ask volunteers to use words in sentences to show the "person" meaning of **ist** and **ian**.

Transfer Rhyming Patterns

- Have students use rhyming words to spell **boil**, **broil**, and **chain**.

81

Lesson 47
thickness

Lesson Focus: rhyming patterns **ice**, **iss**, **ink**, **ick**
est, meaning most
en, changing part of speech
ness, changing part of speech

Letters:
e	i	c	h	k	n	s	s	t

 Make Words: ice nice kiss hiss sink sick tick stick thick think stink nicest/insect sicken sickest kitchen/thicken thickness

Directions: Tell the students how many letters to use to make each word.

- Emphasize how changing a few letters or rearranging letters makes different words. Words that can be spelled with the same letters are indicated by a /.

- Give meaning or sentence clues to clarify the word the students are making:

    "Add 1 letter to **tick** to spell **stick**. Some people call a cane a walking **stick**."

    "Change 1 letter in **kiss** to spell **hiss**. When they get mad, a cat and a snake might **hiss**."

    "Use the same letters in **nicest** to spell **insect**. A mosquito is an **insect**."

    "Use 7 letters to spell **kitchen**. Let's eat in the **kitchen**."

- Give the students one minute to figure out the secret word and then give clues if needed:

    "Our secret word is related to the word **thick**."

Sort Rhyming and Related Words

- Have students pronounce words as you put them in the pocket chart. Then have them sort rhyming words and related words.

Rhyming Words:
ice	kiss	sink	sick	sicken
nice	hiss	think	thick	thicken
		stink	stick	

Related Words: nice, nicest; sick, sicken, sickest; thick, thicken, thickness

- Use related words in a sentence that shows relationship. Point out the "most" meaning of **est** and how **ness** and **en** change how words can be used in sentences.

Transfer Related Words

- Have students use related words to spell **harden**, **hardness**, **brighten**, and **brightness**.

- Ask volunteers to use words in sentences to show how **en** and **ness** change how words can be used in sentences.

Transfer Rhyming Patterns

- Have students use rhyming words to spell **quick**, **brick**, and **slick**.

Lesson 48

wilderness

Lesson Focus: rhyming patterns **ed**, **id**, **end**, **ew**
re, meaning back or again
less, meaning less or without
ness, changing part of speech

Letters: e̲ e̲ i̲ d̲ l̲ n̲ r̲ s̲ s̲ w̲

 Make Words: new red rid lid led end send wild wind wire drew
renew rewind redness endless wireless wildness wilderness

Directions: Tell the students how many letters to use to make each word.

- Emphasize how changing a few letters or rearranging letters makes different words.

- Give meaning or sentence clues to clarify the word the students are making:

  "Add 1 letter to **end** to spell **send**. Did you **send** her an email?"

  "Change 1 letter in **wild** to spell **wind**. My grandpa has an old watch he has to **wind** every day."

  "Use 7 letters to spell **endless**. I was eager to go on vacation and the last day of school seemed **endless**."

- Give the students one minute to figure out the secret word and then give clues if needed:

  "Our secret word is related to the word **wild**."

 ## Sort Rhyming and Related Words

- Have students pronounce words as you put them in the pocket chart. Then have them sort rhyming words and related words.

Rhyming Words: red   rid   new   end
led   lid   drew   send

Related Words: new, renew; wind, rewind; end, endless; wire, wireless;
red, redness; wild, wildness, wilderness

- Use related words in a sentence that shows relationship. Point out the "back or again" meaning of **re**, the "less or without" meaning of **less**, and how **ness** changes how words can be used in sentences.

 ## Transfer Related Words

- Have students use related words to spell **sadness**, **happiness**, **awareness**, and **eagerness**.

- Ask volunteers to use words in sentences to show how **ness** changes how words can be used in sentences.

Transfer Rhyming Patterns

- Have students use rhyming words to spell **stew**, **threw**, and **chew**.

83

Lesson 49

Lesson Focus: rhyming patterns **aw**, **eat**, **it**
er, meaning person or thing

Letters: <u>a</u> <u>e</u> <u>i</u> <u>h</u> <u>r</u> <u>s</u> <u>s</u> <u>t</u> <u>t</u> <u>w</u>

Make Words: art sit hit saw thaw wash shirt straw sweat threat
sister sitter hitter artist washer waiter waitress sweatshirt

Directions: Tell the students how many letters to use to make each word.

- Emphasize how changing a few letters or rearranging letters makes different words.

- Give meaning or sentence clues to clarify the word the students are making:

  "Change 1 letter in **sister** to spell **sitter**. I make extra money being a dog **sitter** when my neighbors go away."

  "Use 6 letters to spell **waiter**. My cousin is a **waiter** at my uncle's restaurant."

  "Use 8 letters to spell **waitress**. The **waitress** brought us all refills on our sodas."

- Give the students one minute to figure out the secret word and then give clues if needed:

  "Our secret word is a compound word and we have made both root words."

Sort Rhyming and Related Words

- Have students pronounce words as you put them in the pocket chart. Then have them sort rhyming words and related words.

Rhyming Words: saw   sweat   sit   sitter
thaw   threat   hit   hitter
straw

Related Words: wash, washer; sit, sitter; hit, hitter; art, artist;
wait, waiter, waitress; sweat, shirt, sweatshirt

- Use related words in a sentence that shows relationship. Point out the "person or thing" meaning of **er**, **ess**, and **ist**.

Transfer Related Words

- Have students use related words to spell **tourist**, **actress**, **princess**, and **hostess**.
- Ask volunteers to use words in sentences to show how **ist** and **ess** mean people.

Transfer Rhyming Patterns

- Have students use rhyming words to spell **claw**, **paw**, and **raw**.

Lesson 50
thunderstorm

Lesson Focus: rhyming patterns **ot**, **ort**, **ound**, **outh**
re, meaning back or again
under, meaning under or without
un, meaning not or opposite
en, changing part of speech

Letters: e o u d h m n r r s t t

Make Words: hot shot sort short storm north south mouth round mound mount remount thunder shorten student unsorted southern undershot thunderstorm

Directions: Tell the students how many letters to use to make each word.

- Emphasize how changing a few letters or rearranging letters makes different words.

- Give meaning or sentence clues to clarify the word the students are making:

  "Add 1 letter to **sort** to spell **short**. It is just a **short** walk to the store."

  "Change 1 letter in **mound** to spell **mount**. The jockeys got ready to **mount** their horses."

  "Use 8 letters to spell **unsorted**. I am creating folders to organize all my **unsorted** documents."

- Give the students one minute to figure out the secret word and then give clues if needed:

  "Our secret word is a compound word and we made both roots."

Sort Rhyming and Related Words

- Have students pronounce words as you put them in the pocket chart. Then have them sort rhyming words and related words.

Rhyming Words:

hot	short	south	round
shot	sort	mouth	mound

Related Words: shot, undershot; short, shorten; south, southern; mount, remount; sort, unsorted; storm, thunder, thunderstorm

- Use related words in a sentence that shows relationship. Point out the "back or again" meaning of **re**, the "not or opposite" meaning of **un**, the "under or without" meaning of **under**, and how **en** and **ern** change how words can be used in sentences.

Transfer Related Words

- Have students use related words to spell **undershirt**, **underground**, **northern**, and **eastern**.
- Ask volunteers to use words in sentences to show how **ness** changes how words can be used in sentences.

Transfer Rhyming Patterns

- Have students use rhyming words to spell **sport**, **bound**, and **rebound**.

Reproducible Letter Strips

1. a e e i c f l p r s _ _ _ _ _ _ _ _ _

2. a e e u r r s s t _ _ _ _ _ _ _ _ _

3. a a e e k l n r s t t _ _ _ _ _ _ _ _ _ _ _

4. a e e c h r s t _ _ _ _ _ _ _ _

5. e i o f k r r s w _ _ _ _ _ _ _ _ _

6. e o b c h k n r w ___ ___ ___ ___ ___ ___ ___ ___ ___

7. a e e i d n p r t ___ ___ ___ ___ ___ ___ ___ ___ ___

8. a a e u l n n p s t ___ ___ ___ ___ ___ ___ ___ ___ ___ ___

9. e i d f l n r y ___ ___ ___ ___ ___ ___ ___ ___

10. e e c f l p r t y ___ ___ ___ ___ ___ ___ ___ ___ ___

11. a o u d g l n p r y

_ _ _ _ _ _ _ _ _ _

12. e o u u d d g n n r r

_ _ _ _ _ _ _ _ _ _ _

13. e e i o m r t v

_ _ _ _ _ _ _ _

14. e e i o g h r t v w

_ _ _ _ _ _ _ _ _ _

15. e i o g h n r t v

_ _ _ _ _ _ _ _ _

16. e i o n n r s t v   e _ _ _ _ _ _ _ _

17. a e o u u f n n r t t   a _ _ _ _ _ _ _ _ _ t

18. a e u c f l l r y   a _ _ _ _ _ _ _ y

19. e o u f l l p r w y   e _ _ _ _ _ p r _ w y

20. e e o l p r s s w   e _ _ _ p _ _ _ w

21. e e i g h l s s s t w _ _ _ _ _ _ _ _ _ _ _ _

22. e e e d f l n s s s _ _ _ _ _ _ _ _ _ _ _

23. a e e b c c l l r y _ _ _ _ _ _ _ _ _ _

24. e o o c c l m r s t y _ _ _ _ _ _ _ _ _ _ _

25. a e e m n r s t t t _ _ _ _ _ _ _ _ _ _

26. a e e e u m m n r s t _ _ _ _ _ _ _ _ _ _ _

27. e e e i m n p r s t x _ _ _ _ _ _ _ _ _ _ _

28. e i o d h n n s s t y _ _ _ _ _ _ _ _ _ _

29. a a e i d p p r s _ _ _ _ _ _ _ _ _

30. a e i o d p p r s v _ _ _ _ _ _ _ _ _ _

31. e i o c c d n n s t   _ _ _ _ _ _ _ _ _ _

32. e e e i d d n n n p t   _ _ _ _ _ _ _ _ _ _ _

33. e i o c c l n r r t y   _ _ _ _ _ _ _ _ _ _ _

34. a e i i l m n p t t y   _ _ _ _ _ _ _ _ _ _ _

35. a e o o b c f l m r t   _ _ _ _ _ _ _ _ _ _ _

36. a e e i u b d l n r s ___ ___ ___ ___ ___

37. e e i i b f l l n x ___ ___ ___ ___

38. a e o l n p r s ___ ___ ___

39. a e e i c c l l r t ___ ___ ___ ___ ___

40. a e e i b c d l p r t ___ ___ ___ ___ ___

41. a e o u d g n r s _ _ _ _ _ _ _ _ _

42. e i o u l m r s s t y y _ _ _ _ _ _ _ _ _ _ _ _

43. a i o u b c n r s t t _ _ _ _ _ _ _ _ _ _ _

44. a e e i o b c l n r s _ _ _ _ _ _ _ _ _ _ _

45. e i i o m n p r s s _ _ _ _ _ _ _ _ _ _

46. a i i i o c l n p s t ___ ___ ___ ___ ___ ___ ___ ___ ___ ___ ___

47. e i c h k n s s t ___ ___ ___ ___ ___ ___ ___ ___ ___

48. e e i d l n r s s w ___ ___ ___ ___ ___ ___ ___ ___ ___ ___

49. a e i h r s s t t w ___ ___ ___ ___ ___ ___ ___ ___ ___ ___

50. e o u d h m n r r s t t ___ ___ ___ ___ ___ ___ ___ ___ ___ ___ ___ ___

Reproducible Making Words Take-Home Sheet